MBA IN ACTION:

HOW YOU CAN SUCCEED IN MAKING MILLIONS

MBA IN ACTION:

HOW YOU CAN SUCCEED IN MAKING MILLIONS

JOHN HORSLER

Matador
5 Weir Road
Kibworth Beauchamp
Leicester LE8 0LQ, UK
Tel: (+44) 116 279 2299
Fax: (+44) 116 279 2277
Email: books@troubador.co.uk
Web: www.troubador.co.uk/matador

ISBN 978 1848766 440

British Library Cataloguing in Publication Data.
A catalogue record for this book is available from the British Library.

Typeset in 12pt Bembo by Troubador Publishing Ltd, Leicester, UK
Printed and bound in the UK by TJ International, Padstow, Cornwall

Matador is an imprint of Troubador Publishing Ltd

CONTENTS

FOREWORD

This is a book about business for business. It has been written and endorsed by business people who operate today, in the real world. People responsible for the survival and creation of thousands of jobs who have to 'make it happen' each and every day.

It is a book that bridges business and education by introducing the MBA models used in the top business schools around the world. These models are used to aid thinking through an idea, plan, action or indeed grand strategy.

Ultimately though, these models can only aid to present and illuminate the fundamentals of any particular business scenario. In the end, it all comes down to good old-fashioned judgement, based to some degree on past experience, but tempered with a future vision. That is where the importance of people, who make these judgements, which can make or break a business, comes to the fore.

Twenty five years ago when I had landed my first managing director position, I sat opposite a much admired and industry wide respected Ford Motor company senior executive. We used to sit and chat regarding the latest management techniques of the day; waste reduction, continual improvement, zero defects, set up reduction, stock reduction and so on, in his cavernous office in Basildon.

This guy was responsible for managing thousands of suppliers to Ford from around the globe, spending in those days billions of pounds. His comment to me that day has stuck with me for twenty five years. He said, **"John, we can talk about new techniques and management fads all day long, but the real issue is people."** He then went on to explain that on an average day he held meetings with four managing directors from Ford's supply base. His verdict was that three out of four were out of their depth. **"So what chance has the UK got to become great again if 75% of our leaders cannot cut the mustard,"** he added. A damning statement on the ability of our leaders to say the least!

Whether that remains to be true today I do not know. However, it does seem to be the exception, rather than the norm, to hear someone talking about their bosses with great admiration for their leadership ability. I suppose that given, even today, there is a general lack of widespread management education and learning, this comment would remain unsurprising.

It is my real hope and passion that this book helps to bridge that gap a little, to help people to help themselves first. This should then assist UKplc in general and the wider population in particular thereafter. Throughout this book you will find continual reference to a business's greatest asset; that is you – the people. It is people who build the culture, innovate the products and deal with customers. At the end of the day they make the profits in order to regenerate and grow. Nurture them with great care; they want and need to impress you. So let them, and occasionally show them appreciation, and you will build a strong foundation for your business.

I hope this book helps to 'whet your thirst' for further knowledge. I have given a list of free management education links from respected schools, such as Harvard and Cranfield, in the appendix of this book.

ACKNOWLEDGEMENTS

There are so many people to thank for their help in the production of this book, without which this would not have been possible. They are Sheila Cameron of the OU Business School, who has been a superb sounding board. She is something of an MBA legend, having been heavily involved in MBA developments in the UK since the early 1980s. Her authoritative *The MBA Handbook* is an invaluable resource. Paul McDonald, Adrian Taylor, Mick Horan, who every day have to practice what we preach. The initial readers who provided valuable feedback, in particular Tony Heard from Thyssen Krupp Aerospace, and Richard Parkes Cordock, author of the best selling title, *Millionaire Upgrade*. Barbara from www.olioscribe.co.uk for her patience in typing many drafts and Jeremy and his team at Troubador for the production and publication of this book. Finally to my closest and dearest who know who they are, a whole-hearted thank you to you all. Let's hope we have created something of use to somebody some day, somewhere.

INTRODUCTION

I was inspired to write this story by my interest in the continual development of education in general and the management and running of businesses in particular. I use my own experience of running businesses and turning them around to illustrate how you can use the MBA models used in the world's top business schools. I hope to show how these models can be actually *used*, rather than just learned, in everyday business life. This is not an academic book nor is it intended to be prescriptive. As my story unfolds you will discover how MBA models can help you to a clearer understanding of the business issues you face. You can use them to analyse the structures and data you already have to refine your strategy. They are not simply classroom exercises. They *really* work if you know how to apply them in the real world.

The story is about my start in life and my career of running, growing, selling and buying businesses. I have been a director of over 40 different businesses mainly in the manufacturing industry but as time moved on, in more niche service-type industries, where you can never forget that the customer is truly king. My businesses have covered a wide span, from aerospace to automotive, and from yellow goods to white goods. The size of companies has ranged from 50 people to several thousand, in both privately owned companies and PLCs.

I want this book to be useful to anyone considering or already doing an MBA and to the general business community. If the story demystifies MBA jargon and injects some humour into business life, then it will have served its purpose. If it actually inspires anyone to study for an MBA or start a business, even more so.

As the story develops different business challenges occur. For example in some businesses cash was the major issue; in others lack of development was the problem and they needed reinvigorating. You will find lessons from real business situations, turnarounds, cash problems, development, buying, selling, merging, and closing companies. These businesses are generally SMEs (small to medium enterprises) and each situation is illuminated by an MBA model. Most case studies at business school use larger corporations such as Amazon and Sony. But many of us work in smaller enterprises and my story demonstrates that MBA tools are as useful, maybe even more so, in SMEs.

The *benefit* to readers is an insight into a practitioner's experience of running different businesses over 30 years, thus providing business education, MBA education and, importantly, how to apply this theory in the real world. It is a story of humble beginnings and the personal gain and loss of serious money. The business world is rarely a one way bet, and this story shares the gains and pains along the way.

The journey draws on my experiences of learning from different cultures, especially the Japanese for their manufacturing excellence. Then, how I started my own business, turned it into a PLC and the pitfalls I found upon doing this. I explain how retiring became tiring. Thereafter I went back on the acquisition trail for fun, clashed swords with the Takeover Panel before retreating back to Spain to lick my wounds. I demonstrate first hand experience of the frailty of our legal system and the lessons to be learned from this. I show how to bring companies out of the ashes and inject new life into them. All this with the MBA learning models used both to illuminate the story and to illustrate how to use the models in the real world. And finally, my experiences as a leader and what I have learned before tackling the question are; leaders made or born; ending with some thoughts for the future.

Many lessons about life and business were encountered along the way and it is a pleasure to share them with you.

Background

My first childhood memories are from when I was about four years old and living in a rather poor area of Luton. Born to an Italian mother my earlier formative years were mainly drawn from this tiny, but fiercely strong, lady born 20 years earlier in Cosenza in southern Italy.

I vividly recall her walking me at the age of five (the start of infant school then) to the nearby bakers at six o'clock in the morning. She would leave me with money every morning to buy some hot, fresh sausage rolls before going off to start her first job of the day at 6.30. She came home at around tea time to prepare a meal before rushing off to an evening cleaning job. So I recall from that early age going to the school playground and playing football and marbles with other kids who were in a similar situation. They were happy, happy times.

I wonder, looking back, if those formative years shaped the person I became. Did they give me values? Make me street smart? Did my mother's work ethic, endless drive and competitiveness somehow shape me? I don't know the answer to these questions. I wish I did. There are many psychological studies, and indeed MBA programmes, which engage with the whole nature vs. nurture argument. They try to understand whether entrepreneurs are born or shaped, or indeed both. There appears to be no conclusive answer as it is far more complex. Needs, desires, ability to adapt, strength of mind all come into play, as do the changes that life brings.

My own common sense tells me however, that people (particularly in their formative years) are shaped and guided by those who they admire, respect and love. So I suspect my mother in the end had a lot to do with what I was to become.

My school years were particularly unspectacular

academically as I generally had no real interest. The school I attended to the age of 15 was not overly blessed by academic achievement either. Beech Hill High School was located some 250 yards from Luton Town Football Club and within a massive ethnic community in those days. The five years at that school certainly flushed out the weakest. The law of the jungle was applied in this generally poor community with its vivid mixture of races and cultures. I learned how to build relationships, became street smart, understood trade-offs and indeed how to survive in a harsh environment.

Of course I did generally attend lessons and I knew then - and now know for certain - the absolute value of a *good teacher*. The only subject that I did well in was Geography and this was entirely due to a diligent, hardworking teacher who had control of his class. He made those lessons interesting, engaged us all and made us feel part of it. A rare individual indeed, I now realise. If only such teachers could become the norm in all our schools to educate our future generation, what a start Great Britain would have. Surely this is the way forward, in a world where we have become too expensive to make simple things anymore.

School soon passed, I was sixteen years old. I had absolutely no idea what I wanted to do then but apprenticeships seemed to be all the rage. Work at that time for youngsters in the UK appeared to be plentiful, with many local firms vying to recruit. The Luton area then employed many people in the automotive industry at Vauxhall, Bedford Trucks and so on. I drifted into a four-year engineering apprenticeship at a subsidiary of British Leyland, one of their many tooling shops, producing, in the main, machinery to stamp out car body panels.

Hardened by my formative school years I was now ready to earn my first wage. By and large they were very happy days. I was free from school boredom, growing up with a crowd of good lads in the Apprentice School, earning money, discovering drink and girls. Life was good - no, great! Generally the apprenticeship went well, and my interest in learning grew through college courses which I finally was energised to apply myself to. I was Apprentice of the Year one year and generally I felt that I had at last achieved something.

A change started to happen within me some time around the age of 18 when I finally started to take in everything around me. Closed shop and union meetings were the norm in those days and indeed the whole feel of the company was one of 'them and us', meaning 'management and workers'.

I recall even all those years ago looking around at the waste, inefficiency, poor motivation and thinking then, 'I could do better than this'. As always though there was an exception to the rule. The company had eight section leaders, each responsible for their own section's output and performance. An apprentice attended each section for a short period of time. One leader stood out a mile from the rest, Kurt Strommel of German origin. Here was a guy who made the work interesting, involved everyone, gave praise where it was due and was Swiss-like efficient. What a teacher. He reminded me of my old Geography teacher, getting the best out of all around him and encouraging personal development. If only that company had more like him I thought, as I reflected on the difference an individual can make. The company limped on, 'them and us' prevailed, people did as little at they could get away with. I knew then that this was not the way forward and I left as soon as my apprenticeship ended, at 21 years of age. Some years later I found out that the company had failed and closed. Inevitable, I thought, at some point. I blamed the management predominantly then and still do today as I believe it is their prime responsibility to *'make it happen'*.

1

ONWARDS AND UPWARDS 1975-1978

I had done my apprenticeship, and now wanted to make rapid progress. I had a kind of plan – in three years I wanted to be a manager and in five years a works manager. So I started looking for the next opportunity and applied for scores of jobs. Eventually I was offered a job as an estimating and planning engineer at a relatively new company in the automotive industry, Carford Engineering. What a difference.

I had moved from sleepy hollow at Leyland into what seemed at the time in this new environment like a war zone. Thankfully my jungle training at Beech Hill High School enabled me to survive the all-important first three months probation. Carford had started out with three employees and 10 years later employed many thousands. The management was aggressive to the point of brutal. Everybody was constantly under pressure to perform. Those that did made progress, and those that didn't, left. The pace, dynamism, growth targets and motivation were set from and driven by the top managers, many of whom were also large shareholders in the company. The culture, energy and sheer 'balls out' nature of the environment was the diametric opposite of my previous experience at Leyland.

Within a month of joining I was introduced to the term 'Ghoster'. This term was used when the company had a major issue with one of its customers. In this first case they demanded some extra components for their Ford production line the next morning. Because the company attitude was never to let the customer down, the engineers, managers, directors, and whoever else could be commandeered, were expected to continue working through the night on the shop floor to ensure that the customer got what he wanted the next morning. This was entirely unpaid work – we were all on fixed salaries. But employees showed good will on the assumption that good will would be returned by the company. And guess what? Because we all felt part of it and were somehow shaping our futures we all bonded and were happy to help.

The engine for growth in the company was provided by fat and lazy competition. Since World War II the western world had become largely consumer-driven to the point where, in some product areas such as automobiles, demand exceeded supply. During the 1960s companies such as General Motors (which owned Vauxhall) were generally in a good place. The Japanese onslaught on the western automobile industry was to come a few decades later with their total quality, value-for-money approach, aided by lean production and revolutionary management techniques. So during the 1960s some large suppliers to Vauxhall Motors grew rapidly on the back of increased car sales. Unfortunately, as they grew bureaucracy increased and they became no longer the flexible, dynamic and quick-to-respond type of supplier that Vauxhall demanded. Enter Carford Engineering. Founded by three hungry entrepreneurs who were local to Vauxhall, Carford grabbed a major share of the action in no time.

Thus during the 1960s and 1970s the western automotive industry was a good place to be, with growing markets, strong consumer demand and new models constantly being produced by the major manufacturers. Everybody seemed to be making money. Indeed it was the era of four hour liquid lunch breaks and heavy out-of-hours entertainment between buyers and suppliers, markedly different from today.

Let's introduce our first widely used strategy MBA model at this point, Michael Porter's 5 Forces. We can use this model to help us understand the structure and economics of the 1960s and 1970s.

MBA STRATEGY MODEL: MICHAEL PORTER'S 5 FORCES DIAGRAM

This model was designed to analyse the forces acting on any given industry and the likely economic benefit for any incumbent or new entrant to that industry. In essence, the stronger the forces for change the easier it is to predict the

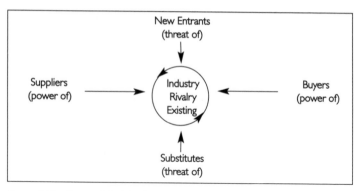

Figure 1. Five Forces Model – Porter

likely economic outcome from that change. If, for instance, there is a strong force from a large number of new entrants to the industry, there is likely to be increased pressure on prices as supply outstrips demand.

ANALYSIS OF THE INDUSTRY USING THE 5 FORCE MODEL

The main players at the time in the west were the American big three – General Motors, Ford and Chrysler – plus the major Europeans such as VW, Peugeot, Fiat and Opel. All these companies were serving a high-growth market. Consumers were demanding more products. The pressures on the companies within the industry were more about styling, innovation and reliability, which in turn to some extent determined their profitability, market share and so on. All companies have their own problems over time but here the general picture was one of the 'quantum of profitability' during the era. The distributorships of these large players also played a significant part in deterring future external competition for some time, due to the availability, cost, and necessary trust that needed to be built between producer and customer. And so the industry '5 forces' model at that time may have looked as shown in Figure 2.

Sketching out this diagram immediately shows the dynamics of the industry at the time and allows us to form a view of the attractiveness (in terms of likely profitability) of joining the industry. In this case all the forces are generally weak, meaning that in general there is no driving force for change in the prevalent structure – so, a good place to be, given that most companies enjoyed profits then.

Over time this 5 force model has been adapted to include two more forces, namely governmental regulation and legislation, and technology. These new forces can of course change the competitive structure of an entire industry. Examples are the technological changes in industry from candles to gas lamps to the light bulb, and government legislation on car emissions (and the tax benefits thereof) driving manufacturers to produce cars with lower emissions to satisfy the customer's desire to pay less tax.

These extra forces display further the simplicity of the model and its adaptability. Of course it is there to be used, adapted and applied as the practitioner wishes in order to

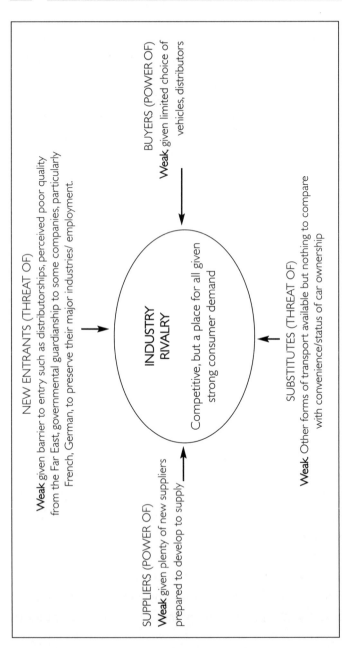

NEW ENTRANTS (THREAT OF)
Weak given barrier to entry such as distributorships, perceived poor quality from the Far East, governmental guardianship to some companies, particularly French, German, to preserve their major industries/ employment.

BUYERS (POWER OF)
Weak given limited choice of vehicles, distributors

INDUSTRY RIVALRY

Competitive, but a place for all given strong consumer demand

SUPPLIERS (POWER OF)
Weak given plenty of new suppliers prepared to develop to supply

SUBSTITUTES (THREAT OF)
Weak Other forms of transport available but nothing to compare with convenience/status of car ownership

Figure 2. Five force model / auto industry in the 1960s/70s

assist thinking strategically about a particular proposition. Indeed Porter's own assessment of the best way to gain a sustainable competitive advantage is to go for a cost advantage, that is be the lowest cost producer, or to differentiate the product through branding or USPs. His own assessment is that unless a company can do this they will be stuck in the middle with the thousands of other companies trying to make a living. I guess this is where most people are in most industries and there good old fashioned sales and service to the customer is king if you are to survive.

At this time Japanese producers such as Toyota, Honda and Nissan may well have assessed the situation while planning their own expansion into North America and Europe.

Carford continued to grow and I too grew into more senior roles, looking around for the best brains to pick within the company to add to my continual learning journey up the management ladder. Then in 1977, married, mortgaged and with our first child on the way I felt another change within me. Life at Carford became ever more hectic as I was by now dealing directly with the senior buying professionals at GM, Ford, Leyland and others. This generally meant long hours, trips abroad, heavy entertaining, but above all making money on the particular engineering new business section that I became responsible for. I loved it. The culture and machismo in the company at the time made me and all those around feel invincible. The competition were nothing. The directors and shareholders who ran the business then set the direction and pace, led from the front and made it happen. They sure did. The growth continued. I became restless however after three years and wanted more and more responsibility. I hoped the rewards would inevitably follow, but first and foremost it was challenge and responsibility that I sought. In my mind I was ready to run the factory, or a factory, and Carford could not provide this, so when a competitor called with a broader role and better benefits it was time to go. And my first company car.

Nevertheless, I never forgot the significance of the culture within a profit-making organization, and the deep effect it can have on success or failure. I learned that if the top of the organization is clear and consistent in its message then the organization generally follows. However, if the top is confused, muddled, spending time on politics, then guess what follows? Common sense I hear you say, but I'm afraid it isn't *common*.

The culture at this time in Japanese companies like Toyota also gives some clue to their future growth. All employees or workers, as we know them, were 'associates' at Toyota. This made them feel part of the company and reinforced Toyota's philosophy of co-existence, co-partnership and co-prosperity. Important words for any new associate. No wonder they grew to become the world's largest car producer.

2

FIRST TURNAROUND 1978-1984

I was now 24 and responsible for engineering, estimating, inspection, tool room, work study and, most importantly of all, getting new work in a company employing some 150 people. The company was part of a public company conglomerate, a 100 per cent owned subsidiary making products for the automotive industry, gas boilers, library shelving and safes. A rather strange mix, I thought at the time.

From day one the place had an odd feel to it. Each product segment was headed by a general manager, four of them in a company with only 150 people. These general managers were each responsible to the PLC board for their own budgets, profit and loss accounts and balance sheets. Daily political infights were the norm as each general manager squabbled for his own share of manufacturing resources, transport, inspection and so on to protect their own personal positions and budgets without any regard for the overall company position. I thought it was a shambles from the beginning. Overall company profitability was invisible except through general hearsay and bits and pieces picked up from the general managers. The culture and the impossibility of getting even the smallest capital expenditure or investment spoke volumes. After some six months in the job the UK entered a deep recession which put huge pressure on our PLC masters. We were told the business was to close in three months as the freehold land that the factory sat on had been sold to inject some cash into the PLC. I was dumbfounded, annoyed, frustrated. I felt I had done my bit and been let down.

Fortunately we were thrown a lifeline. One of the general managers and I were given seven days to prepare a business plan to move part, or all, of the business to leased premises nearby. The challenge was to prepare a plan to resurrect a viable business, one that showed how the costs to set up and move the equipment could be recouped from future profits. Just the sort of challenge I like.

It was probably then that I first learned the absolute necessity of understanding cost control in a business, and detailed analysis of every part. This was to become my very first challenge of a company turnaround.

The company had traded for decades, manufacturing gas boilers, automotive products, library shelving and safes for the government. The company's overhead was massively top heavy with one indirect for every two direct workers. The atmosphere was sullen and uncooperative and the union was strong. General management was weak overall; the attitude at senior levels was one of self preservation rather than focus on the company's needs. Shop floor productivity was below average. Employees enjoyed a bonus scheme that was well beyond its sell-by date, and they had largely abused and manipulated it over time with strong union encouragement. Old, outdated premises with a leaking roof caused constant disruption of production and the flow of goods and products through the factory was massively inefficient. Quality control was reasonable, but not good enough as some defective products were still being returned by customers. Stock levels were huge, with tons of obsolescent stock taking up space and cost and kept on the balance sheet by incompetent managers who had been unwilling to write off these losses to their own P&Ls. Morale was poor and there was a prevailing culture of fear to speak out because of likely reprisals. Customer and supplier satisfaction seemed reasonable. At least some hope, I thought.

Given the closure ultimatum, survival mode kicked in. One of the previous general managers and I, now the works manager of the potential new enterprise, quickly arrived at the above analysis. Just two days into the programme I knew what was wrong. It was now time to put some shape to the new enterprise – its structure, workforce, equipment, products, premises, shop layout, excess machinery to be sold and, crucially, costs, P&L, balance sheets and cash flow for the next three years.

A useful MBA model for understanding a company's position is SWOT Analysis. This simply reviews the strengths, weaknesses, opportunities and threats of any given business in order to assess its attractiveness, or viability, or indeed to help plan the best strategic way forward.

SWOT Analysis revealed the company's profile as shown in Figure 3.

I now understood the previous company's problems, and I had just five days to present a viable business plan to the PLC board to get approval for a phoenix business. The heat was on. To a large degree the SWOT analysis of what was wrong with the current business provided a platform for the new one. The existing company had a sales turnover of £4.5 million with 150 employees. All existing

Strengths	Weaknesses
Reasonable products with their own position in their respective markets. Established company with a thirty + year history. Spread of customers, industries served, giving some diversity, and being less susceptible to a downturn in any particular product area.	Poor general management. Low/no profitability. Low employee motivation. Union power too strong. No effective business or strategic plan.
Opportunities	Threats
Fragmented markets enabling greater market share to be gained by competent management. Stable, albeit mature markets offering opportunity to expand services and products.	Possible loss of market share in its fragmented markets. Lack of profits could force insolvency.

Figure 3. SWOT Analysis

products were reviewed for their gross margin, return per production hour worked and, as expected, some were virtually negative. This provided an opportunity for immediate renegotiation of terms with customers or the cancellation of those products. This was the start base, and I assessed that we were left with £3 million of viable core business that existing customers appeared to be satisfied with and that could be grown over time. From the projected product sales (I figured from our own time sheet records, and by improving shop floor productivity and the bonus structure), that I would need 50 direct employees. We then reviewed the management structure and pared it down to ten indirects to include sales, accounts and administration. This would mean a new direct/indirect ratio of 5:1, a big improvement on the previous 2:1. Sales per head would also increase to £50,000 from the previous £30,000.

Next we prepared the new factory. We kept only the best machinery and ensured an efficient flow of product through the new facility (with no leaking roof), which again would produce both savings and further quality control benefits. Surplus machinery was to be sold off, which would pay for the necessary redundancies, moving costs and disruption. Five days later the plan was put into P & L and balance sheet proformas for the next three years and it was duly sanctioned by the PLC board.

In just three months we had to move all equipment, keep production staff and customers happy and negotiate redundancies with unions – a mighty challenge. But somehow it got done. Failure was not an option.

On day one in the new facility I started a new culture. I turned into a kind of dictatorial guardian. I felt I was being particularly hard on all concerned to protect all our futures. No more kowtowing to unions, although we retained union representation. A fair day's work for a fair day's pay became the mantra. Nobody could hide anymore. Everyone became accountable for their own quality, performance, housekeeping and so on, and everyone was rewarded (or otherwise) accordingly. Meritocracy ruled. I guess my learning in life and experience of the 'Carford Way' set the rules for the survival of this new business, and my new challenge as works manager to make it work. And work it did. The business made money every year for the next five years. There were many sleepless nights and rocky roads to navigate, but I learned that the greatest attribute of successful business people is *persistence*. And the general manager and I scored highly on this particular measure – we would never believe that we couldn't do it.

During my tenure there were many incidents along the way. Change is always difficult and culture can sometimes take decades to alter. I generally met any obstacles head on and tackled them as we went along. One particularly stubborn employee who found the changes difficult was a 6'5", 20 stone, ginger-bearded Geordie. He had been problematic in the previous regime as well. He was the stereotypical forklift driver who believed his job was just to sit there all day waiting for requests to move product around. This he did at his own discretion and depending on who he liked. Ethnic employees (of whom we had many) would sometimes wait hours if this chap so decided. The complaints filtered through to me and the usual employment procedures began – hearings, warnings and so on. Despite his continual protestations he was eventually sacked, at which point he threatened to flatten all around, particularly me. The following day we arrived to find all the office and factory locks filled with superglue. The transport lorries had nails driven into every tyre. I wonder who did that?

This disgruntled employee then appealed to a tribunal for unfair dismissal, which, after months of paperwork and court attendance, was thrown out. He then went to appeal, which was dismissed. Yes, and then on to the House of Lords. Yes, dismissed. Finally the European Court of Human Rights also got fed up with him. Nine months later, after more correspondence and time wasting, he tried to file a civil case. It finally petered out. You just can't please all the people all of the time. Being a relatively small company everyone could see what was going on, and the fact that the company held strong against the threats helped the culture change to stay on course.

Looking back I can see that I too had needed to change, to become something I'm generally not – hard nosed, difficult, sometimes unreasonable, ruthless at times. I also needed to become chameleon-like in order to deal with different situations. Persistence, tenacity, 'can do' attitude, responsibility for all and desire were the attributes I needed to make the venture successful. I had learned something about myself, that I could myself change significantly.

Many companies are only as good as the end products or services they produce. Let's look at the MBA model I used to assess the company's products, the BCG (Boston Consulting Group) Matrix. The BCG matrix allows us to evaluate either a company's portfolio of products or indeed a portfolio of companies within a group.

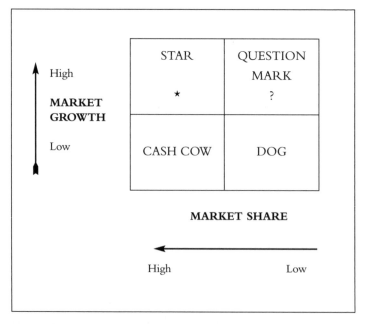

Fig 4. BCG Matrix

The matrix is used to assess the relative merits of products or companies and their existing position. The quadrant showing high growth and high market share is designated a star and should provide good future profitability for some time. The cash cow quadrant gives good profits today but perhaps has a limited life in a low growth industry. Question marks have low market share in high growth markets and so probably need investment and considerable effort to try to move it into the star category. Dogs are generally candidates for divestment or closure as they show low market share and low growth. These are all, of course, generalisations and the model merely illustrates the current position and facilitates analysis of the relative merits of each product (or business) on a case-by-case basis.

Looking at our own four products the BCG Matrix shows a clear picture.

AUTOMOTIVE PRODUCTS were a question mark
They were clearly in a high growth market but the company's market share was tiny. This product needed further consideration.

LIBRARY SHELVING was Cash Cow to Star
Given there were only three main UK players with limited European competition, the company enjoyed good market share. The overall market growth, however, was medium. So the product just about made it into the Star category.

GAS BOILERS were a Cash Cow

Given only four other UK competitors and significant barriers to entry in the form of regulation and safety requirements this product sat in the cash cow category because the market was mature and generally low growth. Nonetheless, it was a good source of continuing cash, for now, and cash is vital in any portfolio.

SAFES were Cash Cow to Dog

A combination of low growth market and low to medium market share required us to consider investment, or perhaps buying a competitor, to increase market share and enhance its attractiveness within the portfolio.

So the portfolio looked something like this – Fig 5.

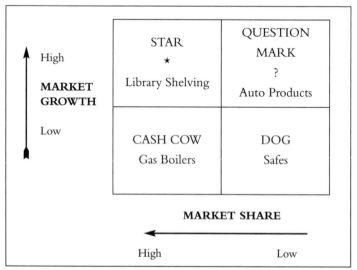

Figure 5. BCG Matrix – Analysis of product segments

The portfolio looks reasonably balanced. Of course more stars would be nice but, beware, in high growth, high market share environments cash can be consumed very quickly. And we all know that in business cash is king.

So here we can see the boilers and library shelving cash cows can perhaps support the development of automotive products into a future star, whereas safes may be a candidate for divestment or closure, or possible acquisition of a similar business to improve its position and move it into a more attractive segment.

This model gives only a superficial, general picture. Much more detailed analysis is required before any business-changing decisions are reached. Its strength, however, is its simplicity. It quickly shows the portfolio strength of a company's products or a conglomerate's subsidiaries, to consider the overall picture.

As it happens the decision to go ahead with the new venture was based purely on economic findings. The BCG illustration however would support the decision because of the balance of the portfolio and its ability to give longevity to its product range, and therefore sales revenues and profits.

This, my first company turnaround, despite its inherent problems, went well. It is never easy. Sometimes obstacles present themselves such as the cost of redundancies or employee resistance to change. It can seem a daunting task but if you do nothing you are probably dead anyway at some point. Change nothing: Nothing changes. If an aircraft is going down the pilot does not have time to ask the views of the people at the back. Somebody has to make it happen, and a key attribute for success must be making quality judgements by considering all the possible scenarios in a business.

I was now 29, and another local company, employing some 100 people, invited me to become managing director. I jumped at it.

3

PROFIT IMPROVEMENT AND GROWTH 1984-1989

I had landed my first job as Managing Director. I felt excited, nervous, apprehensive but above all, determined to make a success of it. I was now in charge, but could I 'cut the mustard'. The company was privately owned and I had negotiated a package of benefits to include a share of the business's pre-tax profits. The business had been operating for many decades and supplied components such as door latches and bracketry to the local automotive players including Vauxhall Motors and Bedford Trucks. A first review of the budget, P & L and balance sheet showed the company to be marginally profitable but with a fairly sound balance sheet. The company had grown steadily but far less than its competitors. Financial controls, and the incumbent accountant were both good. P & L, balance sheet and cash flow controls, done monthly to near audit standard, were in place and this discipline has stayed with me in all my business life since. When you are on a journey without a map you are on the road to nowhere. I also realised at this time the great importance of planning and the significance of asking

- Where are we?
- Where do we want to be?
- How are we going to get there?

Managing directors need to understand the hopes, desires, and wishes of their shareholders, management and employees in asking these questions. And then, of course, map out the action plan and find the necessary resources to achieve it. The maxim of 'fail to plan: plan to fail' is old and well worn for a good reason.

The planning process brings another MBA model into play, the 7Ws:

- Why?
- When?
- Who?
- Where?
- How?
- Which?
- What?

Indeed the concept goes back some time. Kipling's poem in the Just So stories (1902) refers to 5 Ws and 1 H – who, what, where, why, when and how. If each of these Ws is used to question the plan you'll be off to a good start.

After consulting the shareholders about their wishes for the business, (which was continued steady growth but better profitability), I started to set about my own plans (which were much, much more aggressive) as I was on a personal profit share.

Remember that the primary job of a managing director

in a profit making concern is to do just that, make a profit, and sustain it. Two more old maxims highlight the importance of profit: 'profit is not everything – it is the only thing' and 'turnover is vanity, profit is sanity, and cash in the bank reality'. These words have rung true and remained with me throughout.

The business had around one hundred employees and a sales turnover of £4 million. On day one I set about my own plans to improve the business.

INCREASE SALES

I already had many other contacts in the auto industry who I needed to convert into new customers. I set a target of 25% growth per year for 3 years.

FINANCIALS

These seemed generally to be OK, although we needed detailed costings per part to see where the money was being made or lost; even more critical when the mix of work and volumes are constantly changing.

Stock levels and turns were OK and just needed continual improvement.

Debtor day levels were around 40 days, which was fine.

Creditor day payment levels were 35 days. Not fine. Terms

needed to be extended to bring a one-off cash hit back into the balance sheet. After all, I may need this to achieve sales growth, which generally requires more cash initially to fund extra weekly labour costs and additional raw materials.

So financial targets were set: increase creditor days to 45 and reintroduce over £100,000 of cash back into the balance sheet. This would not be profit, just a cash increase achieved by making the working capital work harder.

SALES PRICE REVIEW

I set a target of 2.5% overall increase and started to negotiate with customers. The company had not increased its prices in some cases for 18 months. The sales prices were adjusted so that they were in line with those of our competitors. The target was £100,000 in increased profit as any direct increase in top line sales would flow immediately to the bottom line.

PURCHASE PRICES

I quickly identified that this was a weak part of the business, headed by an even weaker manager. This had to be changed quickly. The spend was £2 million and I wanted 5% savings on this, minimum. Target – £100,000 profit improvement.

LABOUR COSTS

There was a union in place, AEUW as it was then. I forged a deal with them for the next three years fixed at 3% per annum pay increases. This gave the workforce the stability needed without the usual yearly arguments or strikes, which enabled me to do three-year deals with customers knowing by and large what my costs were going to be.

OVERHEADS

I put a complete ban on any more recruitment of indirect staff. When people left the PLAN was to spread the tasks to those who remained, train where necessary and reward them accordingly. Much better for staff morale and more cost effective for the business.

So, taking the existing budget I overlaid my new plan of action. If we could achieve all these small changes the bottom line profitability would increase by some £200,000. I now needed to assess the management team to see if I felt it was capable of delivering it with me. I was as usual faced with the normal scepticism from the shop floor, about my grand plan which was disseminated throughout, to different levels in the company. In any event I initially changed only one manager and gave all the others the chance to follow my lead and *change* or they too would be given different jobs, or in the worst case, redeployed at some point.

Once again persistence proved to be my saviour. During the next three months I implemented the plan. There were of course many difficult times, negotiations and some losses along the way, but overall the plan was a great success and after six months sales were coming from new customers in Europe such as Saab, Opel and Ford Cologne. We were on our way. This significant journey was never entirely without pain I remember. When all around are on the journey each copes differently with the stress. Nobody was forced to do anything but there is sometimes a lot of pain suffered by those involved. At the time it did not appear so important but, looking back, I wish that I had planned better to help those workers who were in real distress. I wish that I had been better at seeing the early warning signals to manage proactively. After all a sick team is no good to anyone.

At the time my only focus was to execute the plan day and night, 24/7. I was in the zone. Nothing could shift my focus on making the plan happen. I truly lived, breathed, dreamt, ate, drank, slept and loved the place. It was my mistress.

After six months, once the scene was set, I devolved more power and responsibility to those who were on the journey with me. This allowed me more time to continue to develop sales and profitability for the next twelve months. I remember one occasion when I was out on a Friday jolly with two senior Ford purchasing officials. My driver picked them up

at around noon and we proceeded to the latest in place to eat in Basildon. Five hours later he would then drop them back to their office for ten minutes to check on any issues or crises. They could hardly talk coherently let alone tackle any problems. I guess that's what about ten pints of lager does. We had arranged to meet later at their favourite Chinese restaurant in Canvey Island where one of the guys resided in a rather large mansion. They were to be accompanied by their wives and various other parts of their families. Freeloaders, these guys were top professionals. The evening proceeded nicely, the atmosphere relaxed. I had known the other family members for some time from previous events. We had now got through about two bottles of red wine each and the brandy glasses were being warmed when one of the guys challenged our latest price increase. We had raised them by 4% and he felt it should have been three. The restaurant was packed, we were completely bladdered and a massive shouting contest ensued. I offered him 'the shirt off my back'. After which I stood up, took my shirt and tie off in the restaurant, gave them to him, put my jacket on and sat down – voila. Cool as a cucumber he put my shirt on over his, sat down and thanked me most courteously. We then sank a bottle of brandy between us and not another bad word was spoken. At the end of the evening we went back to his place for a nightcap. Unfortunately his tipple was large shots of crème de menthe. He put me up

for the night, made breakfast, and then we all went into the Basildon offices to do some business. Not a mention was made of prices. It was just good banter and chat about future projects. I was on my fifth cup of espresso that morning, trying to come round, when I noticed something strange. The Ford executive was wearing my tie from the night before – those guys were unbelievable. But we had a good laugh about it and I guess more goodwill was generated. Those were the days, as they say.

Then in 1986, some months later, a major incident occurred:

The chief executive of a major customer, Ford, representing some 30% of our turnover, declared that he intended over time to source some of our business to South Korea.

Well, just when you think all is going to plan Ford come in to ruin your day. At the time Ford were known to be the most aggressive and difficult people to deal with in the auto industry. I'm sure their buyers were trained to wear 'Hairy Shirts' every day. In comparison at the time General Motors were known as 'generous motors' and nearly went bust before the introduction of their own global sourcing strategy, designed to slash supplier prices.

The Ford plan was to take a skyscraper block in Seoul, South Korea and twenty of the top purchase executives around the world were sent on a two year mission there. The mission being to reduce component costs by switching away from more expensive western suppliers. Their target was a saving of $200 million per annum. They took three of their top purchasing executives to relocate to Korea from the USA, two from Australia, two from the UK and so on. Luckily for me one of the British executives chosen had become a friend over many years. He explained Ford's targets and position over several drinks one weekend and I began to assess the likely impact over time on the company I was running.

I had to go and see at first hand what we were up against given the major impact it would have if we lost the Ford account. I was invited to stay in Seoul at the Ford house where my colleague now resided for one month. It was a large and impressive ambassadorial residence complete with chauffeur, car phone (yes, in 1986) and all the usual trappings. This guy was a purchase agent in Basildon who had been transformed into what seemed like royalty overnight. Of course the Korean government and business leaders were falling over themselves to attract this new Ford business and the jobs and prosperity it would create for their country. So I enjoyed a month being ferried around South Korea, visiting factories that made everything from wing mirrors to glass windscreens, wheels and tyres to body panels. What an eye opener.

Forget health and safety regulations, there was machinery without guarding (guarding slowed the process). Forget sickness benefits (if they don't turn up, they don't get paid). The activity level and pace were at least double that of an equivalent UK business. And given that their wages at the time were one sixth of the UK's, from Ford's point of view the savings to be made were compelling.

As one might expect in an emerging economy the quality levels left something to be desired, but they were improving all the time with Ford's and other major manufacturers' input and training. How could we compete? Armed with the knowledge of this new competition we tried to up our game in terms of productivity and remove cost through better design, but the gap was enormous.

Fortunately for us Ford could not move as quickly as it had hoped. I am still not sure today whether it was, at the time, a political move to get into the country with its vehicles, thus promising future business prosperity by providing work for the Korean suppliers, or whether they genuinely believed the savings were achievable. The cost of retooling parts, and the time involved, proved a significant barrier as the UK suppliers were of course unwilling to stock pile ahead for three months to give Ford safety stock for the transition. There were also major risks to the quality of components as the Korean systems were yet to reach the western standards that were demanded as the norm. As time went on the Koreans demanded

prices that were close to western levels as the Korean economy surged. Korean workers started to strike for better pay and working conditions and Ford's cost advantage decreased accordingly. As the country prospered, and developed its own market, health and safety standards improved, again diluting further their productivity advantage.

This had all happened before, in the 1960s in Japan, which eventually grew to become costlier than the west. It also sounds a bit like China today, although there it will take much, much longer than it took in Japan or Korea to get 1.2 billion people on western wages. In the event some new business for future models which required brand new tooling was placed in Korea, but by and large we escaped relatively unscathed due to the obstacles they faced and the rapidly changing economics and currency in this growing economy.

Given the changes that were happening in the industry it was time to sharpen up our marketing act.

We had three local customers in Vauxhall Motors, IBC (an Isuzu and Bedford Trucks joint venture) and Bedford Trucks. All these companies had new model programmes and, I felt, were ripe for development for more business. At the time Luton Town Football Club was reasonably successful, being well supported within the area. They had just installed a new synthetic pitch and were hiring out the facilities as an extra source of income.

Sitting at my desk one day, thinking about how we could market the business, I had a brainwave. You will not find this in any MBA model I'm afraid. I decided to hire out the Luton FC pitch and facilities and invite all three customers to enter their teams in a mini tournament between all of us. Furthermore, other colleagues in their offices as well as their families could all come and watch from the terraces of Luton FC. It was accepted with emphatic excitement by all parties. I hired a photographer to make a video of all the games, a copy of which was presented to all participants at the end. I had pennants made for each company for the captains to exchange before kick off, together with an engraved cup for the winner.

After the three hour tournament the teams headed to the massive hot baths before joining colleagues and family in the bar and restaurant. A high-quality buffet, free drinks and a presentation of the cup to Vauxhall (the winners) followed. In total some 500 people attended at a total cost for the event of around £4,000 in today's value. The goodwill, camaraderie and sheer fun this event generated was enormous. It has been, pound for pound, one of the simplest and most successful ideas in my career.

At around the same time another brainwave was less successful. One of our customers was a horse racing fanatic. At the time we had a company helicopter at our disposal. It was Derby Day at Epsom and I arranged for the helicopter to meet us at an exclusive hotel in Radlett where we were to have pre-race drinks. We were joined by two others. Off we went to Epsom. Things started to go wrong at lunch in the hospitality suite. This guy could clearly not hold his drink, which apart from making him drunk brought out an aggressive, abusive streak. After he tried to pick a fight with Lord somebody on the table I coerced him out to the track to place some bets. He then tried to pick a fight with one of the Tic Tac bookies, I dragged him away again. The helicopter picked us up, and I boarded with six bottles of champagne for the journey back to Radlett. This chap downed half of one before implying he may spray the rest of the champagne over all of us. I grabbed him and the bottle in a wrestling hold. The helicopter was lurching, the other guests were screaming, as was the pilot. What a bloody lunatic. We landed at Radlett and I quickly got off the aircraft and walked into the hotel. Looking out from the windows in the bar we could see him there, my very important customer flat on his back, lying by the chopper. I still do not know to this day whether he passed out or if one of the others decked him. We left him to sleep it off. Another hour passed before we called the paramedics who finally managed to bring him round. I then poured him into a taxi for our journey to Luton.

It was about midnight as we entered rainy Luton. My customer had gone into incoherent mode. After knocking on doors at three false addresses he had given me it was now approaching 2 am and as people don't like being woken then I was getting more and more worried. Finally I telephoned one of his colleagues at home to get his correct address. When we finally arrived the taxi driver and I carried his seventeen stone frame from the back of the car. I had the head and shoulders, the taxi driver had the feet. It was pouring down as I thudded on the front door with my head. The door flew open. His wife wanted to kill me. What had I done to her poor innocent baby? We loaded him onto the nearest settee and escaped quickly. Five hours later the phone rang at my desk. It was him. He explained that his wife had put a bucket by him which he had vomited in during the night and later managed to roll over in. But other than that he was up at 7 am, cooked a full English breakfast, felt top of the morning, and wanted to thank me wholeheartedly for one of the best days of his life. He was oblivious to the carnage he'd left behind him. Another satisfied customer.

During 1987 and 1988 changes were again happening. The major automotive producers wanted to deal only with larger suppliers, those who were capable of funding and developing their own R & D and of building segments of a car in its entirety. Their plan then was to outsource more and more of the car, and the responsibility for administering this fell to selected suppliers. It was clear to me at the time that if we didn't grow we would be in danger of being so far down the supply chain that we would be unlikely to sustain reasonable future profits. Those companies that were above us in the chain would want a cut of our profits.

We can use Porter's 5 force model to understand the forces

on the automotive industry in 1987. The arrival of the Japanese had significantly increased the pressure on the industry by introducing cut price models, improved reliability and choice. This in turn led the manufacturers to put pressure on suppliers to reduce prices and they would go anywhere in the world to reduce their own costs. Logistics and a rapidly improving internet helped them achieve significant savings. Our products were metal and substitute plastic products (cheaper) were now much more desirable. Many new suppliers entered the industry and the extra competition naturally drove down prices. Buyer/supplier relationships were changing as price became all important and buyers were not reluctant to wield their power. So the economics of the industry were changing rapidly. If we did not change to attempt to alter some of the forces back in our favour then our own outlook looked poor. So in ten years the industry economics had changed dramatically from those depicted earlier.

Over the next six to twelve months I devised a plan which put ourselves at the centre of a network of six other complementary companies that could together make systems for cars (for example to supply a complete braking system – pedal, pipes, chambers, pads etc). I had spoken to the owners of such companies at some length. Each of them faced issues similar to the ones we faced, that is grow or get gobbled up in the food chain of the future. They were receptive to my plan, which was to forge cross-shareholdings in all companies, or buy out where preferred, to create a company large enough to provide systems to car producers and to support a new R & D facility. It was 1988 and the clock was ticking. I prepared for our monthly board meeting for many weeks.

I had analysed, reviewed, planned, costed and listed resources and funding requirements so many times before the meeting that I could recite it almost with no notes. For the next three hours I presented the issues facing the industry and the company, the way forward, and how the plan was to be funded and then integrated post merger and acquisition. I was totally convinced then that it was the only way to go. The board rejected the plan. The company was doing well in their view. I knew then that, despite five long, successful and profitable years for me personally it was time to go.

Personally I felt devastated. It was a difficult time with many sleepless nights. My head was saying stay and my heart was saying go. I went with my heart. I felt that I needed to move outside the auto industry, remain in manufacturing and perhaps apply the models and disciplines I had learned to sleepier industries where they could deliver significant improvements. After much deliberation and many sleepless nights I decided to take on the challenge of being managing director of a recreational equipment designer, manufacturer and installer.

4

PROFIT, DEVELOPMENT, REWARDS
1989-1990

I was now 35 years old and enjoying the trappings of some success in my career and life to date. Money never seemed to be a problem, but then I never craved it either. I guess I wanted a nice car, holidays and so on – who doesn't? But it was never the main driver in those days. That was to come.

And so on to the new venture. I first saw this job advertised in the *Sunday Times* and sent in my CV and letter along with 800 other hopeful applicants. Yes, 800. This is not unusual. In more recent times where I have placed ads we have had over a thousand applications. It can be a real lottery for both parties and business history is littered with MDs who fail within a year. I went through the usual interview, psychometric and graphology tests. The graphology test apparently is able to detect early signs of schizophrenia; an interesting notion I thought. The final test was a case study of a business issue which I was given about two hours to analyze before being subjected to a totalitarian state style of cross examination by the company consultants.

The company was a player in the design, production

and installation of recreational equipment – swings, slides, roundabouts, climbing frames, safety surfacing and so on. It was based in South West England and a subsidiary of a plc. Its major customers were councils, parish councils and government, mainly in the UK but including some previously colonial outposts such as Hong Kong. The company had recently been acquired by a new owner who had put in consultants to advise on change in the business. One of their recommendations was to replace the current managing director, hence my arrival.

Before accepting the position I had researched the company's accounts, competition, products and so on. The new owner's wishes were simply to make more money and to do 'simple things well'. From my side I had agreed the car, salary and holiday package but unusually I agreed a profit share deal only on any upside, so that the company and its owner could not lose. In this case the budget for the coming year showed a healthy profit. If the company achieved only this level of profit then I would not get a penny. However for every £1 over this profit level I would get 10 per cent. Of course he didn't know of the automotive disciplines and strictures of that time and, if applied effectively, the extra gains they could bring to the business.

So on the first day I sat in my newly decorated office pondering the responsibility of leading 140 employees, ensuring their and the company's welfare, whilst working up a one to three year plan for taking the business forward.

I started to notice a succession of heads rapidly walking past my office window. I looked through an adjacent window to see the whole shop floor standing outside the company's entrance gates. Over a hundred of the employees had gone on strike. What a start I thought.

I investigated immediately and discovered that the previous MD had made various promises regarding pay rises which had not happened. Within a few hours I managed to get them back to work with the promise that:

1. If they did not go back to work I would bring in temporary labour to keep the company going; they would not be paid and, indeed, they might lose their jobs.

2. I would immediately conduct a review with management and union representatives with a target date of seven days to find an acceptable way forward for all concerned.

This initial confrontation, I suppose, gives some clues to the previous management of the business. It felt strangely akin to the 'them and us' environment that I recalled from the bad old days of apprenticeship at Leyland. Thinking back, because I had been through that process on the shop floor and knew how it felt, it may have helped me to manage the situation. I knew their likely dodges and smokescreens as well; no-one is ever lily-white in those circumstances. In any event, I just about managed to bring us all together to have a shared destiny in the success of the company. During the next seven days I talked to everyone in the business about my plan. I wanted to expand the business *not* to reduce headcount unnecessarily. I wanted new products, innovation, to remove or reduce waste, and so on.

I have found in business that not everybody wants to be MD; some people don't want *any* responsibility at times. In some ways I guess that's what nature has thrown up; otherwise how would a company function? There are further thoughts on this, particularly the role and lessons I have learned about leadership, in Chapter 12. Somebody *has* to do the more menial tasks; they are an important part of the make up of any business. But one thing that all levels of employee desire, in fact *need*, is security. We all need to pay our bills and look after our families. Some people today still live week to week, pay packet to pay packet, in many factories and businesses across the world. During my discussions I tried to convey my vision for the business and build *some* trust in the workforce out of this the first-day adversity. We agreed a small immediate wage increase which could be augmented further with new quality, performance, housekeeping and timekeeping targets. Well, round one went OK. I was still standing.

During the next seven days I set about refining the company's plan. In a business employing 140 people and with the normal structure of accounts, sales, production and quality manager this is enough time. I have read about people being given three months or the first 100 days to develop their strategy or bring in consultants to advise. Rubbish. If you know what you are doing seven days is plenty for the first cut plan. It will of course need modifying along the way to adapt to circumstances and market conditions generally. I always start by reviewing the existing budget (or, in the absence of one, just doing my own rough analysis).

Budgets are a vital part of any worthwhile MBA programme.

The essential components of a budget are these:

- **Profit and Loss Account**
- **Balance Sheet**
- **Cash flows**
- **Capital expenditure together with justification and appraisals**
- **External finance needed**
- **Explanations of any assumptions.**

I then extend these for three years using assumptions from a sales forecast and business plan. In the 12 month plan I *always* look for the worst case scenario in terms of sales and costs and then do a What If scenario in order to adapt the business if the worst happens, to ensure the resources necessary to survive are in place. From these base components of the budget further analysis can be done, but without the basics in place you simply can't analyse the state of health of any business. I will try to demystify each component in simple terms.

PROFIT AND LOSS ACCOUNT

This is simply an income and expenditure statement which adds and subtracts numbers. The sales output is on the top line, and underneath all the costs involved in making these sales (such as purchases, labour and so on) are subtracted. At the bottom you show a profit or loss for the period whether daily, weekly, monthly etc. If you use equipment that will need replacing over time it is prudent to allow a future cost here in the P & L for replacement; this is known as 'depreciation'. And different rates are applicable depending on the expected life of the asset in question.

It is in many ways similar to an everyday household budget. For example, the equivalent of our sales or income would be our monthly net salary paid into the bank; then our costs will be rent or mortgage repayments, rates, food bill and so on. These costs are recorded against our monthly income. If we expect white goods such as a fridge or washing machine to need replacing in five years time at a total cost of £5,000 then we can allow £1,000 per annum of depreciation within our costs against our yearly income. This then builds up a fund over the next five years so that we can pay for the eventual replacement of these items, just as a factory needs replacement machines every now and then.

So we are all able to produce our own household budget profit and loss account to see whether at the end of the week, month or year we are likely to have surplus income yielding a profit, or if we are spending more than we earn, a loss.

BALANCE SHEET

The balance sheet is used to record the net assets or net worth or shareholders' funds (all the same thing) of a company or entity at any moment in time. It is a snapshot of the assets of the business at the date it was taken.

The household budget example is just as applicable to balance sheets as it is to the P&L. We are all able to evaluate our own personal balance sheet at any point in time. This will show our own personal net assets or net worth. This is illustrated below; this figure shows a personal balance sheet alongside a typical engineering company balance sheet. Consider the comparison.

**A TYPICAL 'INDIVIDUAL BALANCE
SHEET' MAY LOOK LIKE THIS**

BALANCE SHEET

		£	
	Fixed Assets	200,000	House valuation
		10,000	Car valuation
Current	Stock	18,000	Valuation wine collection
Assets	Debtors	5,000	Employers owe 3 weeks
			+£2,000 lent to friend
	Cash in Bank	1,000	Savings
Current	Creditors	(5,000)	Mortgage on House.
Liabilities	payable in 1 year		RBS 20 year loan.
		(5,000)	Loan on car. RBS
Net Current			
Assets		14,000	
	Creditors payable	(95,000)	Mortgage on House.
	after 1 year		RBS 20 year loan.
NET ASSETS		129,000	
Initial	Capital	5,000	
Capital	Retained		
Available			
Savings	Profits/Reserves	124,000	
NET ASSETS		129,000	

Figure 6. Balance Sheet comparison 'Personal and Company'

**A TYPICAL 'ENGINEERING COMPANY BALANCE SHEET'
MAY LOOK LIKE THIS.**

BALANCE SHEET

		£	
Fixed Assets		200,000	Plant & machinery
		10,000	Company cars
Current	Stock	18,000	Raw Material, Finished Product
Assets	Debtors	5,000	Money owed to the company
			by its customers.
	Cash	1,000	
Current	Creditors	(5,000)	Money owed to suppliers
Liabilities	payable	(5,000)	Short term loan
	in 1 year		
Net Current			
Assets		14,000	
	Creditors payable	(95,000)	Longer term Bank Loan
	after 1 year		
		_____	
NET ASSETS		129,000	
		_____	
INITIAL SHARE CAPITAL		5,000	
PROFITS/RESERVES		124,000	
NET ASSETS		129,000	
		_____	

Figure 6. Balance Sheet comparison 'Personal and Company'

You can see that by itemising the values and listing the debtors and creditors this household has a net worth of £129,000 at this particular moment. If the house value increases, however, or you win the Lottery these would need to be added so that the latest net asset valuation is recorded. Why not try your own at this point?

The MBA finance module will also talk about balance sheet ratios. Important ones are 'debtor days' to see if the business is being paid quickly enough and 'creditor days' to ensure you are not paying suppliers too quickly. Tightening these areas helps you avoid using too much working capital in the business. It is much better to turn it into cash to reinvest in other areas of the business, or indeed return to shareholders by way of dividends. It is sometimes useful to compare working capital components such as stock, debtors and creditors against competitors' accounts within the same industry just to see how you are doing. Remember the name of the game is to do the *most* with the *least*. If you are running an efficient balance sheet then you will tie up less shareholder funds or net assets. Any profits which are made in one year can be divided by these net assets to give you your Return on Capital Employed (ROCE) which is another critical balance sheet ratio. This shows what percentage the money invested in the business is yielding. Depending on the risk level in the business, you can determine the return which you require for such risk in the particular business.

The other ratio I like is the Liquidity Ratio, or Quick Ratio as it is known, which is Current Assets divided by

Current Liabilities. This ratio tests the immediate solvency of the company (can it meet its current obligations?). A Quick Ratio of 2:1 is excellent, as there is headroom to pay even if stock is a little slow moving. A QR of 1:1 should be the minimum. Below 1:1 and the company is 'technically insolvent'. There are tens of thousands of companies with QRs below 1:1 that *do* trade successfully. They are just pushing their assets very hard and use the 'Creditors Piggy Bank' to trade.

CASH FLOWS

Using our simple household budget we can project our cash flow for, say, the next twelve weeks. We can use the items listed in the P & L forecast with incomes on the top line and costs listed below to illustrate the timing of cash in and out and thus predict any likely surplus or shortages.

Different businesses will have different needs and some, like airlines with large capital expenditure programmes, will typically project cash flows forward in excess of five years whereas shopkeepers may look forward just a few weeks. But whatever business you are in forecasting cash flow is a vital component of any business if you are going to ensure ongoing survival.

DISCOUNTED CASH FLOWS

Once you have reviewed cash flow for the next three years you can look (you hope) at the free cash flows or surpluses available. Add those surpluses up; let's say it's £100,000 per Annum, £300,000 in total. You can now ask what the value of that future income is right now if you apply a discount to provide either for inflation, cost of capital, rate of return required or a combination of these. That's all it is, as simple as that.

Coming back to the company, once the budget and its components have been formulated and given the once over, I then like to consider the areas for attack or improvement. During the first seven days my overall impression was that we were a market leader in a generally benign market. The company had become a little complacent, with few new products or any real evidence of innovation. Productivity in manufacture was at best lethargic, the existing management structure had its strengths and weaknesses. The competition were little better, although some recent foreign entrants were starting to make inroads. If one considered the business in the light of Porter's 5 forces model, strategically we were in a reasonable place for now.

ACTION PLAN FOR IMPROVEMENT

Sales

The company's sales had been stagnant for a number of years. The existing sales manager was replaced along with two of the existing six field sales managers. This gave a new purpose, focus, and direction to this area which after three to four months started to yield extra sales and turnover.

Purchasing

The existing purchasing team was retained, but with new targets, directives and, importantly, incentives. Usually when any new MD comes in people generally respond and want to protect their own positions. So it is relatively easy to get things changed initially. However to ensure longer, lasting change people have to believe in, and understand, where the company is going and the importance of their own personal role in that journey. I have found that it is vital to relay that to all the key players, and let them disseminate the same message throughout the business. Add to this a fair and achievable incentivised target and change has a chance of being embedded in the existing culture before evolving a new one.

Labour And Overhead

I then set about introducing new quality, performance, housekeeping and timekeeping targets together with a company-wide suggestion scheme which was rewarded discretionally each month in an open meeting with all employees present.

I recast the numbers in each of the above areas after considering in some detail the possible improvements to profits for the business. The targets were:

Sales   +10%   Year 1
             +20%   Year 2
             +25%   Year 3

Purchasing
        Savings 6%   Year 1

Labour & Overhead
        Savings 8%   Gained by doing the
                      increased turnover with the
                      existing labour/hours paid

I also at that time reviewed the selling prices of all products and systems. As we were the market leader the competition generally followed our price rises. The previous MD had not increased prices for two years (despite accepting purchase price increases from suppliers in the same period). His thinking apparently was to drive the smaller competitors out of business. This may be an accepted wisdom but, in this particular scenario the competition was much smaller and even if they went bust others would again start up in a small way. It was relatively easy to get a small share of the market but very difficult to gain a significant stake. So we did some tests. If parish councils were spending a relatively small sum on a new swing then price was seemingly of less importance than reliability, quality of service and above all *safety*. So price increases were implemented on all future projects and, as expected, all our competition soon followed.

It's important to ponder at this stage the effect on the P & L (and of course the benefits to the balance sheet and cash flows) of these improvements. These seemingly small changes added together yield a dramatic improvement to the bottom line.

NEW PRODUCTS, BRANDING AND INNOVATION

The importance of branding and its effect on product differentiation and profits should never be underestimated. Think of the premium prices enjoyed by brands such as BMW, Rolex, Gucci, Louis Vuitton and so on.

After discussions with the company's major customers (local authorities and councils) it was clear that the company was perceived as safe but slightly old fashioned, even boring.

It was at this point that I engaged an outside product designer and advertising company. The designer's brief was to build on the existing range of swings and slides, but to inject some new excitement into the play area. They achieved this by designing touch and light up areas and using learning tools, for example 'noughts and crosses' which could be illuminated for the children. Alongside this the advertising company was briefed to invent a new brand name and logo, and research customers' needs and desires.

Thinking of other companies and their brand development, I recalled Shell Petroleum being replaced by a simple picture of a shell and British Petroleum becoming just BP and I wondered what the designers would dream up for my company. In the end they went for just the first letter of the company's name. With our wallets another £20,000 lighter, we went with it.

It also became clear that the safety of children in the playground was the client's number one concern. The floors of playgrounds were covered with rubber tiles which the company purchased from an existing supplier at considerable cost. I visualised manufacturing these ourselves as the annual cost was over £1 million and increasing as customers demanded further safety features. We found a local tyre-shredding company to supply the granules, mixed in the necessary glue and colouring agent and then poured it into a metal mould. The mould was heated and, hey presto, minutes later we had made our own first tile. We then impressed our logo on to the tile, added various colours, set up a small area within the existing facility, and had reduced overnight our costs from £1 million to £600,000 per annum for a total outlay of £50,000. What a payback.

The marketing module of the MBA programme talks about the 4Ps and product life cycles. The 4 Ps

are product, price, place and promotion. And the life cycle is the natural life of any product before it is substituted by a better or cheaper product.

Let's apply the 4Ps to the products (swings, slides etc) at the playground company. We reviewed our prices against those of our competitors and in many cases (for example complete playground installations) it was nearly impossible for the customer to compare accurately the various offerings, hence our new pricing policy. Place, the distribution channel was through our own sales force of six people regionally spread throughout England selling directly to the end customer, and promotion was mainly through very professional catalogues, selective advertising and the yearly Trade Show. This show cost £40,000 per annum and the company had exhibited for the previous ten years. When we evaluated the cost/benefit of this show I decided not to exhibit and save the £40,000. This again was not the conventional wisdom but the consequence of our non-attendance was interesting. The talk of the whole show, of all our competitors, was our decision not to exhibit and the astonishment it caused. I think we actually got more publicity by *not* attending. I did agree to attend the following year, but at a much reduced cost of £20,000, much more in line with the results our costs/benefits model projected.

The life cycle of the products in the company was extended to say the least. The slide had been around for 100 years. The materials within the product, however, had evolved over time from wood to brass and then to stainless steel. So there was product evolution rather than product revolution.

The old style tube television is an example of the product life cycle. The product is designed, marketed and sold initially in large numbers as consumer demand rises until it reaches maturity when most people have got one and there is too much supply chasing demand. Then fierce competition prevails and prices drop before the product vanishes with the onset of a newer product, the flat screen TV for example.

For the next three months I set about implementing, managing and enforcing all my new budget proposals. Night and day my only focus was to attain all my planned targets for sales increases, purchase reductions and so on. Nobody was going to stop me. I was in the zone. I look back now and I believe I truly was. It was almost a cocoon-like environment I had created within myself. I was obsessed with ensuring that I would not fail. I think this sheer determination and persistence rubs off on all around providing they believe in you, and that you are fair, reasonable, consistent and show that you should indeed *be* the leader. People want to be led, they *need* the security and stability that effective leadership brings. Twelve months on the results show just what you did and how you did it. The results are unemotional, they are the truth. The numbers speak volumes about the actions behind them. We absolutely smashed the budget apart. My own personal profit share for the period was a tidy six figure sum. Back in 1990 that wasn't bad.

Soon after this I was headhunted with a serious incentive package by a public company to help to turn round some of their ailing subsidiaries. After a couple of weeks pondering the future at Sandy Lane Hotel in Barbados (well, you have to have some enjoyment or what's the point?) I agreed to join the PLC world, lured by promises of massive riches and future stardom. The PLC was a group of electrical products manufacturers with a full listing on the London Stock Exchange.

I also decided at this time to enrol on the Open University's MBA programme. Given my poor academic background I felt it was time to actually go and learn how to do things properly. Despite having no undergraduate degree I was accepted on the three year part-time programme. It was to become a life-changing decision for which I will be eternally grateful to that wonderful organisation.

5

CASH IS KING 1991 – 1992

Refreshed by the white sands, clear waters and tropical climate of Barbados I was ready to take on a new challenge. It was 1991 and the UK was firmly gripped in the teeth of recession. House prices continued to fall, challenging the age-old wisdom of the saying, 'as safe as houses'. Unemployment continued to climb, and life in business was ever more challenging.

I had first met the board of the Electric PLC some months earlier at the head office in Slough. The antics here pre-dated the comedy hit 'The Office', which looked pale by comparison. I was the new kid, keen to make an impression and help to revive their ailing share price, and I was given one of the subsidiaries to sort out. This company manufactured heat sinks for the consumer electronics industry, predominantly television sets. These were aluminium components that were placed near circuit boards to draw the heat away from the electronics and hence improve their function and longevity. The business had about fifty employees and was based in Essex, a mere three-hour daily commute on a good day from my home.

On day one I arrived at the company to be greeted by the incumbent managing director who had been fired by the PLC board, and was working out his notice with one month to go. It was here that I truly first understood the meaning of 'cash is king'. Cash is truly the king of business.

After the usual pleasantries I set about a question and answer session with the outgoing MD in a somewhat similar way to the MBA model of the 5 Ws which questions continually Why, Why, Why…

The technique is used to ask a series of questions to try to detect the root causes of any particular issue or problem. The theory being that if enough questions are asked, preferably from different angles, that the root cause of any problems will emerge.

If the issues centre on a more project orientated question, for example capital expenditure for machinery, then the MBA model of the 7 Ws is a more useful technique. This one asks who, why, where, which, what, when and how, to test the validity or usefulness of any decisions made, and rationale thereof.

During this six hour meeting I made copious notes, and tested some of the answers I received by asking the *same* question but in a slightly different way. There was a budget in place which, as ever, helped to provide clues about the problems that needed to be addressed. However, the biggest clues to the operational issues were the three interruptions by the company accountant who was desperate to discuss calls he was taking from the disgruntled creditors of the company. During this long chat I was weighing up this chap, trying to understand his knowledge of the business, trying to ascertain if he knew where the money was made and indeed, crucially, where it was being lost.

In any business where the objective is to make a profit, then you would expect that the guy that is in charge of running that business would be very clear about how and why the business is or isn't profitable. After some brief deliberation, I asked the critical question, 'What is the return per hour the business needs to make a profit, and what do you actually return?'

He did not even know what I was talking about. Then I knew it was time for him to go, which he duly did.

This particular business produced components from the factory floor where there was a number of production hours available to make the products, which in turn generated the sales revenue for the company. In effect their service was selling production hours. To calculate 'the return per hour', if you take the sales turnover minus the production materials used to make those sales (known sometimes as the Value Added in MBA speak), then divide this by the total production hours available, that will be the 'return per hour' required in the budget to give a projected return on sales. The following profit and loss budget example below explains this. The company had 20,000 production hours available.

Sales	£1,000,000	
Materials	£200,000	
Value Added	£800.000	
Production		
Costs	£200,000	Total hours available
		20,000 @ 10/hour cost
Overhead factory		
rent, rates etc	£300,000	
Sales, Admin.	£200,000	
Net Profit	£100,000	10% ROS (Return on Sales)

In this example £40/hour is required, i.e. 20,000 hours x £40 = £800,000 Value Added necessary to yield a 10% ROS.

Therefore all existing business and, crucially, new future business *must* be gained at £40/ hour at least when quoting for new work in order to sustain the 10% net return on sales required. Of course the model can be tweaked to introduce more production hours or reduce some overhead but in general terms the business requirement for pricing new work should be fixed. Everybody who runs a business must get down to this level of detail if they want to fully understand and run the business successfully.

A useful MBA technique when reviewing financials is

'sensitivity analysis', sometimes known as 'what if' scenarios. For example if we take on a contract of say £100,000 but only at £30/hour what will be the net profit be? Or sensitivity analysis could be applied to an overall drop in sales of say 7% in order to assess the likely drop in profits, the resultant effect on cash flows, and therefore the viability and solvency of the business. Banks these days refer to these scenarios as 'stress tests'. They have indeed of late, had their own such challenges to meet. Whatever the business, the challenge is for the MD to get to grips with the key numbers. An accountancy firm, for example, sells 'expertise hours' from the practitioners to clients. A proper budget can calculate the costs of premises, overheads and administrative staff to show what hourly rate is necessary from their income producing employees in order to yield a net profit for the firm. If partners at the firm quote for work under this required level the result will be poor or no profitability.

'All this is so obvious', I hear you cry. I agree, it should be. But in the pressure of the business environment, and sometimes with the difficulty of attracting new business, it is very common for the MD to take their eye off the ball and just muddle on. Even today I am continually amazed when I ask business owners what hourly rate they achieve. Nearly always they don't know. A quick analysis of the accounts tells the true story if you know where to look.

As soon as the previous MD had left I called together the

management team for an introductory chat. My first impressions were that they were generally a diligent bunch. They had been with the company for some time and were pretty hacked off with the group PLC board in general and the newly-departed MD in particular. Their comments being, 'They' don't care about 'us'; 'they are sometimes late paying salaries' (alarm bells started clanging in my head at this one); 'they keep changing the board and we don't know who we work for any more'. These comments, typical in an ailing company, were I felt a cry for help rather than just a general whinge. They came from that all powerful five-letter word 'money' or the lack of it in this case. The first day had now finished, and I decided to stay over in the area for the next two nights to try and get to grips with the matter. In the hotel bar that night I reflected that I was only twelve hours into the new job and Barbados seemed like it was ten years ago.

The next day I toured all the premises, interviewed key managers for about twenty minutes each and introduced myself to all the employees. Down to work. The key issue currently facing the company was cash flow and, as it turned out, it was even more so for the Group. Every day management time was spent on fire-fighting phone calls from creditors chasing payments, with threats of litigation, and winding up orders on the company. The business was in survival mode. My first directive to *all* was that no payments or purchase orders would be valid from now unless they had my signature on them. This gave me control of all outgoings and future liabilities. Looking at the balance sheet I asked for a complete breakdown of the company's stock, debtors and creditors. This shows the working capital of the company, and it was my intention to get it working as hard as possible. Always remember 'do the most with the least' is the name of the game, to improve performance and boost ROCE (return on capital employed). I took a quick snapshot of these key elements (the fourth, cash, was irrelevant because there was none, only the steady trickle in from collection of debtors). Stock seemed quite high, some four weeks of sales value, debtors about two and a half months of sales value, and creditors were being paid on average 90 days plus. I looked at the detail.

CREDITORS

Many companies that get into trading difficulties just continually shop around to get supplies. If they are up to their credit limit with one supplier, they will try the next and the next, and so on until their reputation gets around for paying no one on agreed terms. Then all their supplies dry up. This way forward in my view should only be used as a very last resort, and be a very short term fix which then gets resolved later. Otherwise, the danger is that directors of the company can become personally liable if the business is trading with little chance of creditors being paid. It is called trading whilst insolvent and is illegal.

I reviewed the creditor lists in detail and, as usual, payment terms had been agreed by the key suppliers at 30, 60 and in some cases 90 days. The common denominator in virtually all cases was that the company was trading beyond its terms. I prioritised each case as follows: For example…

- **Essential**: electricity, gas, water;
- **Preferable**: steel suppliers, albeit we could (short term) hawk our business around;
- **Non-essential**: magazine subscriptions, Christmas party fund, new car budget.

From this list I then analysed the amount of cash required now to pay creditors, and get them all back onto normal trading terms. The deficit was £160,000. The number was flashing at me in amber lights. I just stared at it until my mind switched into survival mode. I parked this analysis for now. It had taken about four hours to do, was not perfect by any stretch, but would be within ± 10%, good enough I figured, for now.

DEBTORS

In the balance sheets of most companies the debtors list (money owed to the company by anybody but usually the company's customers), is a significant asset of the company. This means that provided the customers have good credit worthiness (i.e. are likely to pay) then the company can borrow money from banks and use the debtors as security. Normally banks will lend up to 50% of the debtors as an agreed overdraft facility. Since the recent banking crisis banks are trying to persuade companies to use their own factoring services which will, in certain cases, forward up to 80% of the debtor book as a loan. The rationale for the banks is that since the 'credit crunch' banking rules have changed to ensure that they hold more internal reserve capital against overdrafts. This they would rather not do. They make money by lending out.

Looking in detail at the debtor book before me, there was in this case no chance of raising any further loans against it, as the group was itself over the agreed consolidated group loan agreed with the banks. So what to do? I firstly tested any debtors over 90 days (yes there were many) to check their validity. Very often if a company is badly run its ledgers are a mess. I telephoned the top ten debtors over 90 days personally to check why they hadn't paid. Unsurprisingly the main reason was that nobody had chased the debt. Only one debt looked bad – a good quick hit in a few hours. The accounts staff blamed the previous MD who had directed them not to chase customers in case it upset them. Well let's just go bust then, I thought. I then considered the 30, 60 and 90 days amounts that were due from the company's customers. The two largest were long standing customers of some 20 years and I was told relations had been very good for many years. Interesting, I thought. Maybe I could get terms reduced to, say, seven days rather than 60 days. That would definitely free up some cash. But it might also start alarm bells ringing at our major customers so I parked it for now.

STOCK

My initial quick look at the balance sheet had shown the stock value quoted to be roughly equal to four weeks' sales output from the business. This seemed quite high, given the fast moving, short factory process time to produce the goods. It was to be a few years later, when I encountered the Toyota production system in Toyota City, Japan, that I was to learn the real meaning of minimal inventory in a production system. Anyway, armed with the latest stock records under my arm, I walked the floor and the stock with the factory management team.

It soon became apparent that the philosophy here was one of building it just in case the customer may want it, rather than the far leaner Japanese approach of just in time. There were many storage bays holding far too much product, not only tying up money in capital but also the costs of extra floor space, risks of product obsolescence, risks of product deterioration and so on. Taken all together the costs of holding excessive stock are significant. The good news was that most of the existing stock appeared usable, or saleable. At last, I thought, this is definitely an area we can aggressively attack to reduce our working capital and hence get some cash back into the business. The overall value of the stock was £400,000, and if we could halve this over time it would release some £200,000 back into the business.

However this would not come easily. This would entail a

complete culture change in the company; its people would need to think differently. Gone would be the buffers of copious product on the shelves. Gone would be the luxury of suppliers' products ready in place to use when and if required. Strong leadership would be required in order to demonstrate how it could be done, together with the necessary training programmes. Day two had almost ended as I pondered on any other potential assets that might be sold to raise cash, redundant machinery for example. There was none, and as is usual the fixed assets (plant and machinery), property and debtor book, were fully pledged to the group's bankers.

CASH CONVERSION CYCLE

This is the period of time in which a funding gap exists, between the goods being paid for and money being received for them. The ideal situation would be to buy the products in the same month as the shipment. So, if payment is made 30 days from the end of the month as well as payment received for them, there is no funding gap and therefore no/minimal working capital requirements on the balance sheet.

This is the name of the game. To do the most with the least resources, something companies such as Toyota do so effectively with JIT and minimal inventory.

Back in the hotel bar that night, comforted by a few large Jack Daniels, I considered the issues before me. It was just the end of day two and the company was plummeting fast. I had already taken full control of the purse strings, analysed the working capital components, met all of the people in the company, removed the incumbent MD, and sketched a few pictures in my mind of how to pull ourselves out of this mess.

On day three I arrived at the factory at 6 am along with the first shift of people. I think this act alone spoke volumes as word spread, as it does like wildfire in factories, to people arriving on later shifts. Never had the previous MD arrived much before 9 am. Culture change has to be led from the top, and sometimes from the front. At 8 am that morning I addressed the whole workforce. I explained that the company had some major challenges ahead of it, nothing insurmountable, but significant change was required to keep the business afloat. If we changed nothing, nothing would change. I explained that all our jobs were under serious threat of extinction. When questioned about the group position, I countered with the fact that our focus had to be on what we could do here. Provided our own little ship was tidy, profitable and viable, whatever happened to the group this company would be attractive to somebody, and hence give better protection for our own livelihoods. I then got to the crux of the matter, how it would affect them. At that point I had no real handle on working efficiencies and practices, but my past experiences had already made me fear the worst here. It would, I thought, be most unusual for all the noise level, and poor management for this particular section to be super efficient. So for now, I just told them that any overtime from now on would need to be sanctioned by me personally. I figured that with all the stock we had, and our cash flow problem, to pay premium payments on top of our existing weekly wage outflow would have been particularly stupid. Of course this didn't go down well, and was met with the usual cynicism and derision by a small group of employees. I did however state that I did not envisage any redundancies within the programme of change, and that all areas of the business would be under severe scrutiny to get us back on track.

That afternoon I gathered the management team together to outline my emerging plan for survival, to thrash out the issues and (I hoped) build a consensus of support.

The headlines of the plan were as follows:

DEBTORS

- **Action**:
To chase customers aggressively to pay and stick to our agreed terms;

- **Target**:
To get an extra injection of cash estimated at £60,000 within ten days;

- **Action**:
To talk to the Finance Directors of our two largest debtors to offer a discount of 2 ½%, for early payment;

- **Target**:

To get an extra injection of cash, estimated at £125,000, within ten days.

CREDITORS

- **Action**:

To meet with the top ten most important suppliers to discuss payment plans and to share some of the company's future vision;

- **Target**:

To stem any more pressure for immediate cash and to schedule a detailed repayment plan to present to creditors.

I would undertake the task of talking to creditors myself.

STOCK/PURCHASES

- **Action**:

To reduce stock holding. To reduce future purchases and thus liabilities.

- **Target**:

Reduce stock by £200,000 over a six week period.

I would authorise all future purchase orders myself.

SHOP FLOOR/STAFF

- **Action**:
To reduce costs and waste. To minimise or remove any costly overtime working. To improve productivity/ output.

- **Target**:
£100,000 per annum improvement through stronger management coupled with future incentive plan and working smarter.

I had five direct reports and I gave each of them a copy of the plan that evening after we had brainstormed the 7 Ws. This enabled the tasks and responsibilities to be divided. Daily progress reports were to be distributed at 8am every morning.

One month later the cash issues had gone away. Two months into the change programme the business turned a profit. Six months later it was by far the best performing subsidiary of the group. Simple steps applied effectively and managed diligently, that's all it took.

While matters were improving head office politics continued apace. This, coupled with infighting between those responsible for different subsidiaries and their own personal battles to gain some scarce group resources, made life pretty unpleasant generally. Bad news for the PLC and its shareholders. I had been commuting for nearly twelve months now with three hour journeys, plus ten hour days, to watch the profits I made get squandered elsewhere. I was not happy, and I told the group chief executive that I wasn't. He had his own grand plan for change which I reviewed, but the promises I had received when I joined were fading fast. I was losing interest quickly.

During my two and a half year absence my previous employer (trying to get to grips with the ever changing automotive industry) lured me back into the fold with a group directorship and even more lucre. It was an easy decision.

My MBA studies had started, it was not easy. Having had little previous academic study experience I initially found the Open University three year part time MBA programme a huge challenge. The first year was mainly general business studies such as human resources, organisation studies and accountancy. Most of the study was home based with occasional classes, augmented by online learning, and a seven day summer school was mandatory. This was my first taste of university life. I attended the Heriot Watt University in Edinburgh that summer – what a fantastic experience. We were split into teams of six for the duration and we learned, presented and competed with the other teams on particular case studies. In my own team we had an architect, an NHS manageress, a City of London care manageress (battered wives refuge) and a consultant surgeon. What a mix. Before attending summer school we each had done our dreaded assignments and received our marks. Two significant things happened that very first day at summer school which have stuck with me for nearly twenty years now:

To get to know each other we were paired to review a business question, and give a possible resolution. I was paired with the lady who ran the battered wives refuge. After we had both thought about the business question, we prepared our suggestions to present to the other pairings in the class. This lovely lady spent the next five minutes explaining to me in some detail how she saw the issues. You could have knocked me down with a feather. I was gobsmacked – talk about two different people approaching the problem in completely different ways. She was analysing the problem with a focus on softer human issues such as health, welfare and wellbeing – not a mention of profit. At the time I thought she was mad. However, over the next few weeks I learned a lot about life, and different management styles from this woman. What an eye opener.

I was then paired in the afternoon with the consultant surgeon (only thirty two years old). Our first gossip was about our marks for previous assignments. He confessed to me that so far he had failed. He was mortified, as he had only found out one week before summer school. Why? He simply had not answered the assignment's questions with reference to the *course material*. He had read the assignment and given his own theory on the answers. It was probably a brilliant paper, but with no reference to the course material it received minimal marks. This guy was the most brilliant mind I have ever met but he had made the fatal mistake. Needless to say, when he finally understood the rules of the game he got brilliant marks. I never fully understood the rules until after my MBA, when I was to teach the subject for a short while. The way the system works is that a professor reviews the course material and sets a question. Against this set question the professor will sketch out a model answer, and a suggested marking scheme for references to certain course models used. So when the assignments are sent to tutors for marking they are marked against this scheme. The tutor is then policed by more experienced markers for marking fairness, and this is how the degree is regulated. I just wish somebody had told me that at the beginning of my studies, rather than leaving me to find out for myself at the end. If you know the rules you can work with them. Nevertheless that wonderful institution, the OU, brings together that diversity of all backgrounds in life, to share and enhance learning experiences – fantastic. A bit more on this later.

Now onto my next venture, where I would again have to tackle the automotive industry and cross paths with governmental departments, Japanese competition, the DTI and its prolific peer Rt. Hon. Michael Heseltine, a 'proper' politician and leader.

6

LEARNING JAPANESE 1992 – 1995

The company had engaged a headhunter to recruit 'the best in the business'. They ended up with an MD who had a first class degree in engineering from Cambridge University but, I was later told, little idea of how to manage, hence his departure and my arrival. This is an all too common mistake in business. The decision makers get blinded by brain power. Of course it helps to be intelligent in business, but this is only part of the make up necessary to make it happen.

Attitude, need, desire, persistence, tenacity, drive, 'can do', nous – these are the real attributes necessary for success. Intelligence without these (and crucially the ability to get on with people of *all* levels) is resigned to academia in my view.

My task was to bring the company back to profitability. It had slipped badly during the previous two years, somewhat unsurprisingly given Porters 5 force model study of the economics of the industry. I reviewed the budget together with the last two years' management and audited accounts, a story of continual decline. The monthly company board minutes gave a flavour of what was being said, major decisions made, and so on. Discussions with the management quickly revealed that they had become de-motivated. I formed the view that the previous MD had been out of his depth. It was, I think, a case of the head of an organisation being muddled, and muddle being what filters down – not a good business scenario.

A quick review of the economics of the industry did little to raise inspiration. General Motors (having nearly gone bust themselves a few years earlier) who were a major customer, had put a new gun in charge of their global sourcing. This chap headed a task force with a mission to 'buy anywhere in the world for the most competitive price'. And so overnight the company's competition had gone from the normal dozen or so in the UK, to potentially thousands, manufacturing in much lower cost bases around Europe and the world, for example, Poland and Brazil.

The industry 5 force model analysis looked painful. Industry rivalry was intense and many new entrants meant lower prices. Substitute products were also increasing, with the use of plastics for vehicle lightness and the general picture was difficult. Price increases (despite inflation at 3 to 4%) were non-existent and, indeed, price decreases became the norm, just to retain existing business levels.

And so, what to do? Clearly efficiencies needed to be found, and quickly. Overheads had already been pared to the bone. Higher sales would also help, but where from? Other industries? New customers? Maybe a smallish acquisition?

The next seven to ten days was spent brainstorming these and many other issues with the management team to try and ascertain the best way forward. During these sessions I started to introduce some MBA concepts to aid our thinking, sometimes to immediate direct effect and sometimes not so. However, it is surprising what can jump out from brainstorming, different scenarios, sometimes the best ideas. One such **MBA model** we used in order to think about the wider or macro level economics of the industry was **PESTEL**, an acronym for political, economic, social, technological, environmental and legal issues that can be reviewed to help assess future potential issues in a given industry. Let's see how just one of these, technology, can work.

TECHNOLOGICAL CHANGE

Automobiles since the start were made predominantly from steel, with lately some aluminium for weight reduction. Plastics had been used many years previously because of its low weight, anti corrosion properties and ease of manufacture. But the company's only area of expertise was the production of steel components, and to try to diversify into plastics wasn't feasible without significant investment. Increasing petrol prices meant that consumers wanted more miles per gallon from their cars.

Governments were also concerned about car emissions around that time. Weight reduction of the car would enable better mpg and also aid the development of electric hybrid cars, and hence reduce future emissions. Plastics answered these issues to some extent and better forms were continually developing. In fact year on year metal components were being substituted by plastic components on a car by around 4% per annum (remember Porters 5 force model). This can all be considered as a technological threat to the future of the business. In any event, what was clear was that the business needed a change of direction.

Somehow the company had to become more efficient, and somehow increase sales revenue to return to profitability. Around this time in the early 90s the UK government was becoming increasingly concerned about the future of domestic manufacturing so a number of initiatives (such as trade fairs and trade visits) had been introduced. The DTI at that time, led by Rt. Hon. Michael Heseltine, came up with a 'learning from Japan' manufacturing initiative. Honda, Toyota and Nissan were by now all successfully making cars in the UK, and the government was keen for all manufacturing companies to learn, and then implement, Japanese manufacturing and quality techniques to become more efficient. If only I could get the company onto this scheme, I thought, surely it would help to drive further continual improvement through the company. I filled out the application form that night.

I then got sales revenue with our existing customers under

my microscope. New customers were always welcome, and sought, but this would be part of a more medium term plan because of the time it takes to nurture and bring new business on board. I considered the landscape or 'macro environment' in MBA-speak. General Motors, our main customer, demanded, no *needed*, lower prices for its own survival. They had their own manufacturing plants around the world, and for each one there was generally an established local supply base supplying panels, axles and so on. The car market for new build around the world at the time was approximately 40 million. This broadly broke down as 13 million in Europe, 14 million in the Americas and 13 million in Asia. (Today these numbers are starting to alter, with the fast development of the Chinese, Indian, Russian and Brazilian markets. The BRIC countries, as they have become known.) I focused on Europe for now. The UK market was about 2 million, Germany 3.5 million, France 2.5 million, Italy and Spain around 3 million with the balance built mainly in Belgium. I always found it useful to consider the macro view to help think through the bigger picture. Any external developments can be considered using PESTEL analysis as we have seen. The number of cars produced at the time matched somewhat unsurprisingly the number of cars in fact sold in those countries. They correlate to some degree to the population of the countries, UK roughly 50 million, Germany 80 million, France 65 million and so on. The demographics in developed countries, as ever, dictate to a large degree the size of this and many other consumer products. I then considered the relative cost bases of my competitors in those countries, and at the time it was as follows:

Production Costs/Country 1991 Automotive Components

- UK   £1.00
- WEST GERMANY   £1.40
- FRANCE   £1.35
- BELGIUM   £1.30
- POLAND   £0.40
- CZECH.   £0.40
- EAST GERMANY   £0.40
- SWEDEN   £1.60

These were the labour, social and overhead costs. Raw materials (steel) were roughly similar. The exchange rates used to compare were a mixture of current rates and the futures market prediction.

No wonder General Motors were shifting business eastwards as fast as they could. However, France, West Germany and Sweden, led by their own high cost social programmes, were now way above production costs in the UK, and so a sales strategy was born.

I had been at the helm for about a month now. The first month's profit forecast looked awful, and was further deteriorating. I had now cast a vision in my mind, and called the management team together to talk through our plan. The three headings and targets were as follows:

SALES REVENUE INCREASE

* 20% per annum

* Target: General Motors Plants Europe
  Sweden – Saab
  Germany – Opel
  France – Opel

SHOP FLOOR/
COMPANY WIDE EFFICIENCY GAINS

* 20% improvement per annum

* Target: Apply and get acceptance to the DTI 'Learning from Japan' initiative.

MANAGEMENT/COMPANY WIDE MOTIVATION
20 New ideas

* Target: To distribute the plan through all levels within the business to make everybody feel part of it.

From this initial briefing and discussion each manager was given seven days to come back and present his detailed action plan for making it happen.

It became known in the company as the '20 Plan'.

I personally took charge of getting acceptance on the DTI scheme. After many tests including interviews by the government's consultants (Andersen Consulting) we were finally accepted. We were then given a full insight into the manufacturing and quality techniques of all the Japanese UK producers, Honda, Nissan and the mighty Toyota.

This was followed by visits to the suppliers in Japan to see their own philosophies, efficiencies and culture. The Toyota Consultants at Toyota City in Japan explained in great detail the Toyota production system (which today has iconic status given Toyota's vision at the time). I took as many people as they would let me on those tours.

Back at base the works manager was tasked with implementing techniques which generally centred on waste reduction, for example zero defects in the production process. Indeed every month a section of the workforce – yes operators – were asked to present to the company their latest efficiencies for the 20 plan. It proved motivating to all.

About six months into the programme, and given that we went at it full on, we were visited by Michael Heseltine and his entourage. After the usual factory tour we decamped to the local hotel, where a group of shop floor workers gave a full presentation to the head of the DTI and other government officials, on the improvements the company had made since the 'Learning from Japan' experience.

I sat back and listened to these shop floor workers presenting to the highest level, and I still think today it was one of my proudest moments in business, to see how people if given the right encouragement and opportunity can raise themselves way above even their own expectations. It was amazing. Thankfully all the others were similarly impressed and after the usual press photo sessions we all got back to reality, work. We had a business to run.

We had weekly update briefing meetings to check our progress on the action plans. After a few months things were improving, but not at the rate needed to produce our own targeted 10% net profit on sales. We had made contact with all the General Motors subsidiaries and received enquiries. We had indeed been more competitive on many quotations we had done (particularly in Germany) I discovered from senior UK colleagues. But it was proving a difficult nut to crack; the Germans can be intransigent at times. Unsurprisingly some of our UK competitors were on the same track and by and large had given up. Persistence again was our saviour. The main decision makers for the German business were based in Russelsheim (about an hour from Frankfurt). So I booked myself into the local hotel frequented by the purchasing managers after a quick crash course in basic German. I had set up as many meetings as possible during the next two weeks, I was at the bar every night, basically as entertainments manager, during which at least I got to know them away from their ingrained, day to day, cultural environment at work. I seemed to get accepted, to a point, and we received many more enquiries but still no orders. Finally an enquiry came through which I could afford to take on at a loss (without it being a major problem to the business). I went in even under the Polish and Czech prices, and yet still there was reluctance to place the work in the UK. Armed with the knowledge that ours definitely was the most competitive bid, I started to bang as many doors down at GM in the UK and Germany as possible. Finally we got our first order and then the flow continued; maybe luck, definitely persistence. Our other UK competitors couldn't break through. A lesson learned though; somebody has to make it happen. Persistance, persistance, persistance.

During the next few years the company returned to profitability. Life in the automotive industry continued to be challenging at all levels – price, service, quality. But I was generally feeling that my job here was done.

My own MBA studies had gone well the first year, and I was now well into my electives (strategy, project dissertation, finance/marketing and manufacturing for strategic advantage). I attended any tutorials available and loved the one week Summer schools based in different institutions around the country. One such University, Trinity College, Dublin, slipped my grasp as I could not make the particular week. Remorseful sigh – maybe one day I will go back. All that diversity of experience, the sheer exuberance and thirst for knowledge was invigorating.

Then, as all seemed to be going well, a major

shock. I think John Lennon once said 'Life is what happens whilst you are making other plans'. I now faced the first real tragedy in my life. I was 39 years old. It was my birthday, and that was that very day my father died at the tender age of 58. Reflecting now I think that this event brought about another change within me. Despite the prognosis coming some months earlier the eventual shock and heartache would take over a decade to ebb to acceptance. From that day, 'celebratory' days such as birthdays and Christmas meant nothing any more. I was told that would change over time – it hasn't. I think then, and even more now, why not make every day the 'best day of the rest of my life'. An old maxim, 'tomorrow is owed to no one', rings true. The best piece of simple advice I have ever received, whether in sport, business or life, is to think positively. If you think negatively guess what you get?

I think the events before me, and the approach of the dreaded forty, gave pause for reflection. I sat and pondered. So far I felt as though I had been blessed. I had come up through a fairly poor (but dearly loving) family, with generally low academic qualifications, but somehow managed to carve out a fairly successful career.

My career to date had also brought with it the trappings of success. Interesting word – 'trappings'. I had travelled extensively around the world on business and on holiday.

Money never seemed a problem, but then I was never looking for the problem either, only opportunities. My MBA studies finally finished, and I was ecstatic to find out that I had passed with Distinction. This kind of life check got me thinking about a life strategy. Where am I? Where do I want to be? How am I going to get there? And thinking these questions through I decided that I had finally had enough of working for other people.

I was now on the lookout for my own business. I felt energised, with all the previous troubles now behind. I searched the business sale agents, FT and accountancy firms to put feelers out. I telephoned all my previous contacts. I felt a new change from within. I had had enough of working for somebody else. I had done my apprenticeship, running other people's companies. I had done my MBA. I now craved to run my own show and, yes, for the first time I felt I wanted to make money for myself, lots of it.

7

FIRST GO AT MY OWN SHOW 1995

I had definitely decided to take the plunge, but plunge into what? No more working for somebody else. I was met with the usual resistance from my wife (who by nature is totally risk averse), which after constant discussion gradually broke down into a kind of acquiescence rather than full on agreement. In short I pledged only to gamble savings made and not offer the family home as security on any new venture. I guess her point of view was, why bother? Our lifestyles were first class, money was never an issue; it was hard for her to understand. For me it was dead simple; I just had to do it.

Looking back I think the importance of getting agreement from one's family when starting a new venture should not be underestimated. There are always tough times, especially in the beginning, and support from loved ones can make or break during the inevitable difficult periods. I had put out as many feelers as possible and initially cast my net wide in researching the type of business to go into; then analysing costs, risks and rewards for each. My initial list included restaurants, bars, property development and, of course, engineering and manufacturing companies.

During the next seven days I visited as many businesses as possible to try to find the right new venture. They all had their pros and cons, as all businesses do. Nothing is ever easy in the business world. All businesses have their own problems. After much deliberation I finally decided to buy a 50% share of an engineering company. I decided, after looking around, to take the advice of the now well-known management guru Tom Peters by 'sticking to the knitting', sticking to what you know best, particularly if it is a new venture.

The consequences of owning less than 51% of the issued share capital (i.e. the majority and therefore control of the company) should not be undertaken lightly. There are several potential issues in play. I will explain.

A LESSON IN BUYING A SHAREHOLDING IN A PRIVATE LTD COMPANY

All private limited companies have a Memorandum and Articles of Association. Basically a set of rules for operating the company which can be altered with the agreement of the shareholders. Therefore anybody buying into, or indeed buying the issued share capital of any private limited company, should study these rules and procedures carefully to understand any quirks which may be there. The two companies I was buying into were manufacturers of manipulated tubes, used on automobiles (brake pipes, engine pipes, petrol filler pipes and so on).

The chairman of the company was selling me 50% of the issued share capital, I was then to become the managing director of the company. Aha, equal rights I hear you say? Nearly. The 'Mem. and Arts.' (abbreviated colloquialism) stated that in the event of shareholders 'deadlock' the chairman was entitled to a casting vote, which effectively enabled him to implement unilaterally certain plans that he wished to carry out. As part of the purchase process of buying the 50% share I had this clause removed to ensure that our shares of 50% were indeed equal in all respects. Never just rely on solicitors to pick this up in the sale and purchase agreement. Some will, some won't. It is too important to leave to somebody else. Therefore beware if you own less than 50% of a private limited company, potentially the only future buyer may be the majority shareholder. Of course this is a generalisation. If the future plan of the business is to go for a public flotation, or there is a clear exit strategy for a trade sale for example, then the minority shareholder may be comfortable with his position. However, in all cases where an equal or minority stake is purchased it is essential to draw up a shareholder's agreement. Then agree a set of rules for the future, on matters such as remuneration, future sale of shares and pre-emption rights (giving existing shareholders the first option to buy other shares). In this, my first 'personal' purchase, I made sure the share sale and purchase agreement, shareholder's agreement, and Mem. and Arts. were drafted in accordance with my requirements.

The main manufacturing business was based near its main customer in the West Midlands. Its sister company, based in Leicester, supplied cut tubes to the Northern site. The owner at the time was a strapping ex-rugby player (6'5" and twenty two stone) who had been instrumental in founding the company some twenty years earlier.

As we have already seen times were generally tough in the automotive industry, and it looked as though they were getting worse. So why this one, I hear you ask? Well, I was first introduced to this business by an industry contact who thought they were going to go bust. Indeed, my future partner, who was then in his 60s, had been hawking the business around the trade for the previous three to four months. As profitability and cash decreased, the significant personal pressure on him increased. It appeared that the interested parties were just waiting in the wings, hoping to pick up the business much cheaper after it had gone bust. This scenario certainly did not suit him, particularly as he had given personal guarantees to his bank to secure the company's overdraft against his private assets.

My initial analysis of the business took three to four hours. I toured the facilities while conducting a question and answer session that revealed some strengths and weaknesses. Remember SWOT analysis?

The strengths of the business were its excellent engineering capability. The current owner was himself a first class engineer, and it showed through into the manufacturing facility. The very reason it had kept a good order book was the innovation in the business.

The weaknesses of the business were (apart from the lack of profit, cash, and a dodgy balance sheet), that the place was in chaos in terms of organisation with people running around everywhere. High noise levels, phones ringing, customers on site trying to get their supply of product. Management morale was on the floor. No wonder all the other prospective purchasers had walked away. Despite good engineering skills, the company organization was poor, being kind.

The opportunity of the business was that risk could be highly rewarded. The business had sales of £10 million per annum, no profits and 200 employees. If I could get this right the potential reward for the money I would risk could be a significant pay off. It felt right.

The threat to the business was immediate extinction unless things changed, and fast.

And so, after all the exhausting negotiations with banks, lawyers, accountants, tax advisors and vendor, I set about the businesses. I had handed over a deep wad of my hard earned cash and made the leap from employee to owner (well 50%). I was determined not to fail. I had to work fast though. The banks had extended facilities for another ninety days to enable a turnaround to happen. If it did not, it was curtains.

Before handing over the dough I had a rough idea of the issues that lay ahead. With £10 million turnover and 200 employees the company had only £50,000 sales per head, the industry average being around £80,000. The cost of the raw materials used for production across the industry was around 40% with ± 5% depending on the particular product made. Here it was 40%, bang on average.

I have always found it useful when reviewing a company's performance (particularly if I am investing in it) to just take a quick helicopter view. It can prove illuminating. During the negotiation process I had allocated about four hours to do some desk research on the company and its competition. I had gathered the names of six competitors, all UK based (the product did not travel well globally). Within an hour I had all those companies' accounts for the previous five years in front of me.

Most companies are 'limited liability', and thus are obliged to file accounts at Companies House. These accounts then become public record for all to see. The idea is that if company directors can enjoy limited liability, normally limited to their original share capital in the company, then the creditors of the company should be allowed to check the accounts of the business and verify for themselves that the company is creditworthy.

Using Companies House records and a credit agency, I could see before me the competition's financial performance during the last five years. The headline averages were: sales per head £80,000, material costs 40%, average salary per head £20,000 being 25%, and therefore a gross margin of 35% to pay for insurance, rent and rates etc., leaving a net profit of around 6%. This quick four-hour analysis had provided some comfort. If the competition could produce these results, then why shouldn't the company I was buying into. The problem may be anything from productivity to poor quality or sales prices but all were potentially fixable.

The next day I called the management team together to brainstorm the issues before us, and to consider any potential solutions. This would give me a first look at the knowledge, capabilities and the strengths and weaknesses of the management. Managers from the quality, accounting, manufacturing, sales and engineering functions were asked to give their own account of what was wrong.

It is worth considering the MBA model Forming, Storming, Norming and Performing in group discussions on future plans/strategies – see fig 7 below.

This is the theory, in practice it is usually whether good, clear leadership emerges which determines the success of the group. But, if you are going to gather a group together it may be helpful to bear these stages in mind to serve as a guide for how your group is developing

I think 'functional' came through loud and clear in every

This is the widely used MBA model first developed in 1965 by Dr. Bruce Tuckman to explain the stages a group goes through when working together on a plan. These stages involve:

FORMING - getting to know one another, a leader normally emerges.
STORMING - team members vie amongst each other to contribute.
NORMING - a consensus amongst the group is established as deadlines loom and the leader takes control.
PERFORMING - the team is now working well together as a whole.

Figure 7. Forming, Storming, Norming, Performing

manager's assessment of the issues. None of them even considered the overall issues of the business, and the effect of their particular function's contribution to the whole, whether positive or negative.

The previous owner was steeped in engineering and was doing a brilliant job at just that function. It was clear the company lacked leadership. It needed a conductor of the orchestra. The meeting continued with some of the usual squabbles between manufacturing and quality, and sales and engineering, without really getting down to the roots of the problem. What did come through in the meeting very clearly was that these people *cared*. Obviously this was to be expected, given that their own potential livelihoods being at stake. But it was more than that, much more. There was a real passion for the company, its products and customers. You could feel it, and see it in their eyes.

I reflected that evening on another MBA model, one that helps us to analyse the motivation of employees, Maslow's Hierarchy of Needs.

Abraham Maslow, a sociologist, in the 1940s categorised all human needs into five levels in the form of a pyramid as in the diagram below.

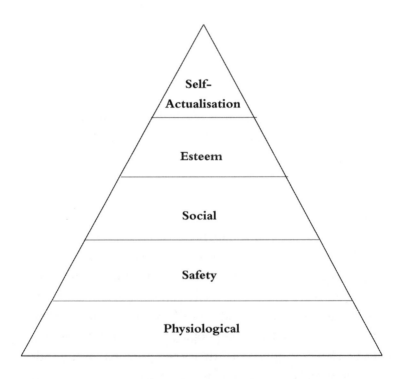

Self–
Actualisation

Esteem

Social

Safety

Physiological

Figure 8. Maslow's hierarchy of needs model

PHYSIOLOGICAL needs:
being the essentials to survive such as food, shelter, water.

SAFETY needs:
such as job security, a safe physical environment and stability.

SOCIAL needs:
such as friendship and interaction with colleagues.

ESTEEM needs:
such as self respect and the need to impress people.

SELF ACTUALISATION needs:
for a sense of purpose and achievement.

Maslow's study suggested that human needs started from the base and then went up in order of further need to eventually get to where you really want to be – achieving something. He concluded that all the steps along the way need to be met before 'self actualisation' can occur. Certainly my own experiences to date have shown that people need security, they strongly desire stability, and thence the ability to make their own way in life.

The brainstorming session I had just held had certainly borne out the desire for *safety* in Maslow's Pyramid. I was already sensing that we were heading towards a crisis and in that particular environment physiological and safety needs definitely came first. However, the esteem and social needs may not be quite as important as actually getting to the self actualisation, and getting things done to personally survive and fulfil the lower pyramid needs of safety. In these circumstances I have found social and esteem needs sometimes get sidelined, and people do have to get brushed aside sometimes. Somebody has to make it happen for the very survival of all. Therefore, while I think Maslow's model does help think through the needs and desires of one's work colleagues to help them and the company to progress together, in a crisis, things can't be so neatly packaged.

The very next morning I stood before the management team with a whiteboard behind me and felt tip in hand. I sketched on the board the critical issues in large letters and numbers.

£50,000 SALES PER EMPLOYEE PER ANNUM

The number in bright red was flashing before us all. It signalled *danger*. The managers looked mystified. I then proceeded to give a quick demo of our competitors' numbers, before asking what was causing the comparative shortfall. Between us we listed the following possible causes:

- **Sales prices too low**
- **Productivity per employee too low**
- **Factory organization and efficiency poor**
- **Pilferage of product**
- **Quality poor and scrap levels high.**

Pilferage and quality were quickly discounted as the product was of no use to anyone other than the company's customer, and the internal quality records and customer returns were more than satisfactory. So we set about a tour of the factory. It was chaos – so many people running around and creating a lot of noise and dust but with no real evidence of any efficiency. I asked to see the top five products by sales value and volume, the highest revenue products. These five products did in fact represent nearly 80% of the company's annual sales, as Pareto's 80/20 rule suggests they should. After two hours analysing the sales price, material and labour costs of these products a trend emerged. Sales and labour costs both needed addressing, and later that day a plan was hatched.

SHOP FLOOR

The headcount in recent times had swollen. The company was currently using agencies to supply seventy temporary employees. This, in itself, is never a good long term solution as labour turnover tends to be high among agency workers, and so company loyalty and care generally can flag. The shop floor was also poorly laid out, with very inefficient product flow. The challenge was to reduce the headcount on the shop floor by 70 employees over the next 14 weeks. This was done by removing all temporary employees with no contract with the company. We could do this by reorganizing the shop floor every weekend, (when there was no production) and introducing certain systems from the Toyota production system such as Set Up

Time reduction and Kan Ban, but even more importantly, by working much harder and smarter than we had previously. A champion was given the job of meeting this challenge, which would be monitored daily for progress by all of us. The champion was the previous owner.

Now, with only one focus for the previous owner, the plan was met in 12 weeks – remarkable.

SALES PRICES

Together with the engineering manager I then set about analysing all the company's sales prices to determine which were losing, and which were making money. It took two weeks, and the results reflected the headline monthly management accounts. As usual it was a mixed bag of good, bad and ugly. In an environment where price *decreases* were the norm, our request for a price increase to our main customer was met with derision to say the least. In fact I was beginning to think we were the good, bad and ugly without the good. However, we had done our homework. We knew our competitors' cost bases and we pitched our new pricing structure competitively. Where necessary this was applied to all our customers. During the next eight weeks we met and talked to the buyer then the purchasing manager, then the purchasing director and finally the managing director of our customers. Each time they tried stalling tactics, threat of legal action and so on, until finally I decided to do what the electricity board does if you don't pay their prices, cut off their supply.

The company had no choice. It either received the correct prices or it would have gone bust. We took this stand with all customers where prices were too low.

That certainly focussed their minds after the posturing of the previous eight weeks. This action naturally caused certain re-actions from some of the more intransigent customers. One large manufacturer had set its legal team in motion, and within 48 hours we had both been served writs (the size of bibles) at our homes at 6 am in the morning. Their lawyer had somehow joined us personally in the legal action they were taking against the company for raising its prices and threatening not to supply if this was not met. Talk about put the frighteners on you. Furthermore, they had managed to persuade a judge to place an injunction on us forcing us to continue to supply at the existing prices for the next seven days, after which, both sides could make their own plea to the courts for their own case. The action at the time was not unusual. It was designed to frighten us off. Indeed if they could have carried it off, we both would have been bankrupt. This type of legal action is rather more frowned upon today since the Lord Wolffe reforms, which require all parties to act reasonably. Our own legal counsel had advised us that we were entitled to raise our prices if we wished. We had no binding contract to suggest that we could not, and furthermore we could not be joined personally to the action as we were directors of the company and acting only in its best interest. Nevertheless I insisted on getting a second opinion from a QC barrister in chambers at the

Temple in London. He confirmed the accuracy of the advice we had been given. Meanwhile some customers were continually threatening to move work away, and not pay their bills which would give us a serious cash flow problem. The following two weeks seemed like years, and two hours of rest a night was all I could manage. Anyway, after all the infighting, squabbling lawyers and general unpleasantness, common sense prevailed. Once our customers had got over their own self-perpetuated price decrease culture and checked our new prices against the competition they realised that we were not being unreasonable. We found an amicable way forward for all parties. Phew! We had achieved our badly needed, and hard fought for, price increase in the end.

Now only three months into the new enterprise we could clearly see a profitable way forward. The forecast sales per head were now £100,000, even better than the competition. Another three months went by and the company was starting to do well. The bank in particular was very pleased and had started to leave me alone. The industry was beginning to take notice of the turnaround, and companies that were interested in acquiring it when it looked like it was going bust started to emerge once again.

We were now becoming an acquisition target, from some larger players and competitors and their executives had contacted me to register their interest if the company was available for sale. My view then, as it is now, was that there was no harm in talking. So during the coming months we met potential buyers.

It was amusing how each went about their own way of acquiring companies. They were all expected to sign a confidentiality agreement to ensure that sensitive information would not be divulged to third parties, and with the usual restrictions on poaching our customers or employees. In exchange we gave them an up-to-date brief resume of the business and its potential. Our first meeting was with TIB who had sent over two of its senior executives for a chat. Well, these two chaps looked (and acted) more like civil servants than senior business executives. They were 'stiff upper lip' types who kept in touch regularly. Gleaning further information along the way before reporting back to the hierarchy PLC board about their progress towards making an offer. From our side we just let this run.

Then the top team of Junior PLC invited us to dinner for a 'chat'. This one just turned into a drinking competition, company vs. company, and my partner at 22 stone could stand with anyone. At around 2 am in the morning they tried to conduct a question and answer session on the company's strategy. The next morning, armed with hangovers from hell, they went off to consider how much they were going to offer, so they said.

Later that week the Fred's Autoparts (USA plc) team turned up at my office, led by their UK chief executive who turned out to be quite a character. The way he carried on I thought he had brought the cash in his briefcase with him. After a while they departed and left it to the parent company's acquisitions specialist, whose job it was to just wear me down with death by a thousand meetings. We decided to just let it run for now.

The fourth entrant into the ring was indeed the chairman and chief executive of Valbonne PLC. He told me that our companies would make a perfect marriage, and that they 'fitted like a glove' with customers, markets and facilities.

With so many possible deals I did the inevitable, sought tax advice.

A LESSON IN TAX MINIMIZATION EXPERIENCE

We were convinced that the most likely purchaser for the business was Junior PLC who would not have required our services post acquisition. As is common practice we sought both personal and company tax advice with a view to paying as little as legally possible. At the time the law allowed that if I were to work abroad in Belgium for at least a year the capital gains tax that I would have to pay would be minimal instead of the forecast 35%. An old contact of mine, in a senior position at Yellowgoods Belgium offered me a job as a consultant to their manufacturing operation, at a low wage of course. I couldn't have it all my own way. Eventually this was not to be, so what other options could be considered?

Around that time several capital gains tax reduction schemes were being touted by the large accountancy firms. They effectively meant buying capital losses in failed companies to offset against capital gains being made. The deal being that instead of paying 40% tax we would pay nothing to the treasury, and 15% to the advisers once all was finally accepted by the Inland Revenue (plus, of course, the usual adviser's fees, legal fees paid up front, to ensure their own costs in the scheme were fully covered). A consortium was set up called the Berger Trust which effectively purchased huge capital losses from a previously failed construction company in Canary Wharf. The company was registered offshore and all the advisors had received counsel from top London barristers who had confirmed that (in their opinion) all was perfectly legal and that the scheme would provide a loophole against current tax legislation.

Along with many others with large capital gains I purchased these losses with the aim of offsetting future taxable gains. Five years later. After many hours wasted, and copious correspondence guess who won? As usual it was the Inland Revenue despite all the previous advice from lawyers, accountants and brokers. As it seems with all these schemes dreamt up by tax lawyers and accountants, they always insist on their own full fees being paid no matter what; they cannot lose. I and others who were part of the scheme then had to pay in full our capital gains tax plus five years interest to the Inland Revenue.

I think several lessons can be learnt from this:

- **In an important decision in life or business never just take advice from only one source. I have always taken at least three opinions on the same question in addition to doing my own research before making a final decision. I have found time and time again that when you try this on some complex issues you will often get conflicting advice from people in the same profession.**

- **If something looks too good to be true it usually is, particularly if its promoters get paid no matter what.**

- **Regarding the tax, do the usual things such as giving shares to your family to utilise their annual capital gains allowances. Maybe invest in some Venture Capital trusts or indeed your own EIS (Enterprise Investment Scheme) company in order to defer some of the gains. But my advice is to *just pay it* and get on with your life.**

The next six months flew by. We were gaining new customers, and I had replaced some staff and recruited a graduate trainee to build for the future. The company was doing well, and the previous customer clashes were now long forgotten. The companies who were looking at possibly acquiring us were all still playing 'cat and mouse'. The first to show its hand called a meeting to present their offer. I was gobsmacked. Several months previously they had signalled an 'indicative offer', subject to due diligence, and the new written offer was exactly *half* of that. What a waste of everybody's time. Well, it was goodnight Vienna on that one.

Another suitor then made a fair and reasonable offer, only to withdraw it three weeks later because of a 'change in strategy'. A three week strategy change? A third offer initially followed the track of the first we had received by offering half, and then increasing by 10% per month forward to try and secure a deal. This became tiresome and we felt unprofessional, so we let it go at month two.

The fourth suitor had rallied support in the city to raise cash to support the acquisition. The company was listed and the chief executive had a substantial shareholding. Our company's customers were complementary to theirs, the new management team looked good and held personal stakes in the company. It was an easy story to sell.

We spent the next two to three weeks considering our futures. My partner was now over 60 and probably a little keener to do a deal than I was at the time. I was to become group managing director, and he would become the group engineering director upon completion, and final acceptance by the acquirer's shareholders.

I spent the next few weeks talking to the acquirer's major shareholders, predominantly venture capital funds and the story for merging both companies became compelling.

The chairman was very well educated and spoke about six languages. I was an experienced managing director, MBA qualified, and my partner one of the most respected innovative engineers in the industry. We would all be significant shareholders in the enlarged company (as we had our own money invested). The multinational customer base became enlarged, as did the manufacturing capability and service to customers. The City loved it – it was the perfect marriage. Or was it? I then negotiated some pre-sale dividends to take advantage of tax treatment prior to completing the deal, and we both duly agreed to the proposition.

The prospectus was prepared by the acquirer's corporate advisers and we were subjected to interrogation by their lawyers about our past, swearing affidavits and becoming familiar with the Yellow Book, the rules and regulations for public companies. Some due diligence was carried out by both parties to satisfy all the shareholders concerned, and then we all duly signed. In a stroke we had both made enough to retire comfortably.

It was a Friday night and we both went out and got absolutely bladdered. That weekend I sat and reflected on the last eighteen months. I had taken the jump from employee to owner, conducted a company turnaround, clashed swords with some multinational customers, had been served a writ (for the first time in my life) from a leading law

firm which could have bankrupted me, had been served with an injunction for the first time in my life, negotiated a company sale with a number of potential buyers, then finally agreed a sale and purchase agreement some two hundred pages long. On top of this from Monday onwards I was to become the group managing director of a public company, a pretty 'hairy ' period in my life. All this and now on to the 'perfect marriage'. Is there such a thing in life? We shall see.

8

MARRIAGE, ACQUISITIONS AND MURDERS 1997

Yes, you read the chapter heading correctly. History is littered with chief executives going on breast-beating acquisitions that have significantly destroyed shareholder value.

It was the first meeting of the new board of the company, held (as were all future meetings) at a rowing club boardroom on the banks of the Thames. The meeting was convened to formalise the strategic plan. The company now had around four hundred employees with sites in the north and south of England. The acquiring company's profits were much lower than ours and this needed addressing. There was also duplication of both sales and accounting functions. The city had backed the deal and they were hungry for share price growth. And so the plan emerged:

- **Organic growth of 10% p.a. sales revenue**
- **Acquisition growth 50% p.a. sales revenue**
- **Centralise sales function – cross-fertilise customers**
- **Centralise accounts – save on costs and centralise the group purse**
- **Improve the profitability at the southern sites.**

The plan was set. The structure of the organization then followed, together with detailed action plans to actually make it happen.

I think it may prove useful at this point to introduce another MBA model that is used in acquisitions and merger analysis – The Parenting Fit Matrix.

The matrix enables you to visualise a business unit's 'fit' within the overall corporation, and to consider its current position, and any future position that it may aspire to. The categories are as follows:

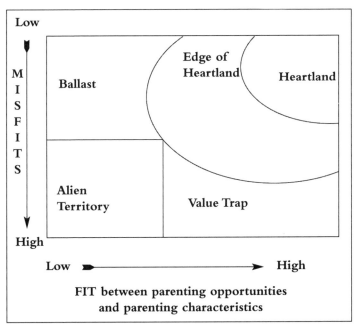

Figure 9. Parenting Fit Matrix

HEARTLAND BUSINESSES

These will be at the heart of the corporation's future. They should have opportunity for improvement by the parent. They should have priority for all corporate activities.

EDGE OF HEARTLAND BUSINESSES

These are companies in good markets but that require continuous review by the parent to either improve or upgrade. If a parenting fit cannot transfer them to the heartland then divestment may make more sense.

BALLAST BUSINESSES

They sit well in the corporation, but have little room for parent improvement. They might be a cash cow in a maturing market but may also hold the danger of slipping into alien territory.

ALIEN TERRITORY BUSINESSES

With low potential for value creation, these are clear candidates for disposal or closure.

VALUE TRAP BUSINESSES

The corporation needs to take great care with such a unit. It fits well, but if, in a niche business needs to be nurtured and care exercised to ensure that it retains its 'niche'.

We can use this model to consider the acquisition. The fit was:

- **Improved overall management for the parent.**
- **Widened customer base for the parent.**
- **Improved profitability for the parent.**
- **Cost savings by centralising sales and accounts.**

So there is no doubt that, using this model to evaluate the acquisition, it definitely sat within the heartland of the corporation, because the parent could improve its situation considerably.

If one goes back to the BCG (Boston Consulting Group) matrix, you will see some similarities to this model. The two dimensions of the BCG matrix are Market Growth and Market Share. But the categorization of the business units into *stars* – maybe *heartland, dogs* – maybe *aliens, question marks* – maybe *edge of heartland* and *cash cows* – *ballast* does show some resemblance, particularly when deciding whether to invest, divest or close. There is absolutely no reason not to use both models if they help analysis and decision making. Anyway, back to the real work of executing the plan.

Because I knew our previous business inside out I decided to camp down at the Southern facilities for the first week. The reported profits there were around 3% net, compared with ours of well over 10%. During that week I walked the floor, day by day, meeting the new people, observing, taking notes, looking at the pace of production, quality and scrap levels, controls in place and so on. I was never quite sure how good old fashioned metal bashing could quite fit into the environment of leafy Sussex. Now I could see why. The culture, 'the way we do things round here', was markedly different from the Northern facility, and not in a good way.

By the end of week two I had finished my analysis, which in general listed actions to be taken on work rate, work organization, material flows and shutting down one of the Southern sites, consolidating into one unit. The forecast future profits from the one site would then bring the overall performance up to the required level.

I was the group managing director and a significant shareholder. I presented what was a seemingly simple plan to gain the board's approval. However, it met resistance. The acquiring board would cite 'city considerations', 'need for caution' and 'measured outlook' until I submitted. And, of course, up to a point they were right to be cautious.

The plan was put aside for now. Although structurally we were not right – the engineering director got cracking to improve the engineering side, as did I on general productivity. Things were improving, albeit far too slowly for my liking.

The first six months flew by. We had made two further acquisitions – a turned parts company for the electrical consumer and construction industry, based near Manchester, and a metal pressing company making products for the white goods industry, based near Bristol. Both had been funded from internal profits, generated mainly by my previous company. We centralized sales and accounts, changed the managing directors, and they started to contribute to group profits and, more importantly, earnings per share which would drive growth in our share price.

In our division of duties on the board, the chairman and the financial director took responsibility for the monthly management accounts, and the six month annual report. I called a meeting with the chairman, FD and my previous partner. Between us we owned about 50% of the issued share capital of the company so you would think we would all have a vested interest in the company succeeding. At that meeting I tore into the numbers and continued until I had gained acceptance to close one of the Southern sites and consolidate as I had wished to do six months previously. This action did not sit well with the acquiring board, although they did acquiesce in the end.

The cultures were so very different. The chairman had set the way things were done there. The manager mimicked him, some talked his way, others even dressed like him. But he had a 'let's see tomorrow attitude'. None of these fitted with our own culture. I have previously mentioned my belief that the culture of an organization determines its success. In my view their culture had to change to succeed.

Let's look at another MBA model on culture, the cultural web which was devised by Johnson and Scholes in 1992.

ELEMENTS OF THE WEB

The theory is that the six interrelated elements help make up the culture (or paradigm as it is called here) and that if you analyse them together you can identify the prevailing culture in any organization and compare its fit with

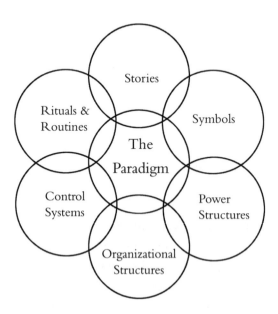

Figure 10. The Cultural Web – Johnson and Scholes

another organization that you may wish to merge with to consider 'cultural fit'.

STORIES

Past events, legends perceived in the company. Communications with each other, customers and suppliers.

RITUALS AND ROUTINES

Behaviour and actions of employees. What is deemed acceptable? Sloppiness, lateness or strict timekeeping?

SYMBOLS

Presentation of the company – plush offices or spartan? Formal or informal dress?

ORGANIZATIONAL STRUCTURE

The family tree published, the unwritten power, and influential players in the company.

CONTROL SYSTEMS
Financial systems, quality control procedures – are they loose or tight, and what values are placed upon them?

POWER STRUCTURES

Key power holders, their influence and direction.

The purpose of the model is to analyse the current cultural position, in order to help you to plan the cultural position you require in the future. In my experience this is easier said than done, and the larger the organization the more difficult it becomes. Cultural change can take many, many years and several changes of management in a company. It has to be driven from the top, every hour of every day, and consistently to stand any chance of change becoming permanent.

I could sit and analyse the cultures of the two companies against each of these headings. Indeed, perhaps I should have done so before even agreeing to our merger. We would have learned something. However, I am not so sure the model, even fully developed, would properly illuminate the cultural differences between the two businesses. The model cannot account for human emotions or 'hidden agendas' in every case. There was clearly a major clash of thinking on the board. I and my partner were action orientated and the chairman and FD being change averse. They were protective of their own culture. And I suppose if their culture had led to a strong successful company, then I, of course, would have worked with it. But it hadn't; far from it.

We closed one of the factories, despite last minute pleas. The culture clash was coming to a head. Maybe it was a case of pugilist versus purist (I was a natural fighter). I guess all marriages come with certain risks attached and despite our radically different business philosophies I respected his views. But in my heart I knew a divorce was imminent.

Operationally things were improving somewhat, and I had brought in some new blood to try to inject some urgency. This worked in part. I was, however, becoming less and less enthusiastic about life in a public company, the measured responses required, and continual reporting of numbers and events to all and sundry. So after about fifteen months I decided that I had had enough and decided to leave the company. I first told my old partner, who was having similar feelings and decided to resign also. The chairman, on receiving our resignation letters, did not want us to work our notice or pay compensation either. A legal spat ensued which, as usual, ended in compromise. I didn't care, I was *free*. It was December. That Christmas I felt three stone lighter, never happier. The burden of continually grappling with the politics, the concerns over numbers, the negativity flowing from the culture had been stifling me for too long.

I was reborn, I was free. I went out and bought a brand new red Ferrari. I had, as a supplier to Fiat (the parent company), been invited to view the Ferrari facility in Modena, Italy, some years before. What a place. What a brand. All employees seemed to love working there, they were so passionate about the company. And marketing – how about this for simplicity? On every new model made the marketing department would work out the

worldwide annual sales for the car. If the number was say 500 cars, then the Ferrari philosophy would be build 499, so that there is *always* someone in the world who wants one. That's what I call keeping it simple, or to use another MBA acronym KISS, Keep It Simple Stupid!

9

SPANISH BLUES 1998

Christmas had come and gone. In the cold, crisp chill of the New Year air I was once again wondering what to do with my life. I was now 43 years old and seriously considering retirement, and so I flew out to Spain. I had spent the previous fifteen summers down in Marbella, enjoying the sunshine and golf, pondering whether to buy or build a holiday home there one day. I now had the time and money to do just that, and set about looking at land, building projects, villas, and so on. Of course this was all in between sunbathing, playing golf most days and drinking a bottle of gin most nights. During the next six months (staying at the Marbella Club Hotel) I felt I had truly contributed to the Spanish GDP. Indeed during that 'hazy' period I think I got to know nearly every bartender in Puerto Banus.

Some things never change though as I was still addicted to reading the *Financial Times* every day. And there was an engineering company with a full listing on the London stock exchange that I had taken a punt on – Backwater Precision PLC – some time before. The company's share price was now trading at 10p per share and with only 40 million shares in issue the stock market was valuing the whole company at only £4 million. The annual report showed that the company had sales revenues of around £35 million. The company was showing losses, but maybe this was fixable. I had to find out more, and flew back to the UK the very next day after arranging a meeting with my stockbroker in London. He had advised that he could buy a block of 2 million shares, 5% of the company at 10p per share, which I duly instructed him to do so. Anything over a 3% stake is announceable to the stock exchange and the public company concerned. Indeed it would be recorded in their future annual reports. I then set off to the company's registrars to find out who the other significant shareholders were: a retired director held 20% and another businessman 10%.

After the stock exchange announcement of my stake I was invited to meet the incumbent managing director and view the facility in Croydon. I was not impressed by the management. However, the business itself looked like it had potential, but only in the right hands. The next day I contacted the retired director and speculator, as between ourselves we could speak for 35% of the company's shares. They were both unimpressed by the performance of the company, and both said they would welcome a major change there, particularly if I personally got involved given my previous track record of running businesses. Over the next week, on the strength of what I believed was an agreement to get change into the business, I continued to set about a plan for change.

I then contacted the board to call a meeting with their chairman. I explained that I now spoke for 40% of the shareholders of the company and requested two board seats, non-executive directorships for myself and the retired director. The idea being that we would act as *agent provocateurs* to the existing executive directors, rather than the normal non-exec role of helpful acquiescence. And once inside with full view of the facts we could start to get things changed. This all seemed to be going to plan but, meanwhile, the incumbent managing director was busily smooching the retired director with his own deal. When the retired director then told me he was now not interested in any changes, I was truly lost for words. They say never trust anyone in business; those words were ringing in my ears.

So now we only had 20% of the shareholding, a markedly different number. We had over 10%, and could have called an EGM (Extraordinary General Meeting), but that probably would get nothing resolved.

I knew this company could be brought back into profit in the right hands. The way I saw it £35 million sales and, say, £3.5 million profit and on a stock exchange P/E ratio (Price/Earnings) of 8 then the value of the company would be £3.5 million x 8 = £28 million, which divided by 40 million shares in issue gave 70p per share, seven times what I had bought for. To say I was frustrated would be a major understatement.

I wrote to the board outlining a plan forward. The lawyers got involved but with only 10% held personally I was going nowhere. I had been back in rainy old England for over a month now, and was beginning to miss the sunshine. So after offloading some of my shareholding I flew back to Marbella to lick my wounds.

ACTING IN CONCERT

I had just enjoyed a marvellous lunch at the poolside grill of the Marbella Club Hotel when I took a call on my mobile. It was from the Takeover Panel of the Stock Exchange. I was stunned. The rather well-educated voice on the other end was demanding a meeting regarding events around shares purchased in Backwater Precision. They apparently had contacted the retired director and speculator already and so I flew back to London for a meeting at the Stock Exchange. The company, through its lawyers, had apparently reported the three of us to the Stock Exchange, accusing us of 'acting in concert' to try to takeover the company. In the rules and regulations of the Stock Exchange anybody who builds up a personal stake of over 30% of a public company is obliged to make a bid for the rest of the shares in that company, normally at the highest price the bidder has paid for the shares in the previous twelve months. This is Rule 9 of the City's Takeover Code. And equally it is frowned upon if, say, three individuals who know each other set out to buy, say, 17% each of a public company and then, once they have a combined 51% of the business, take control of the company. I certainly had not been 'acting in concert'. I did not even know these individuals before. I had certainly contacted them in order to try and influence change in the company, but that was to benefit shareholders anyway. So I turned up at the meeting in one of the walnut-panelled offices in the Stock Exchange and the atmosphere was distinctly frosty. The temperature soon rose however from the grilling I received from the investigating officer. After about four hours, and once I had explained all my share transactions and meetings, I was given full clearance and an apology for the trouble I had been caused. This fell short of agreeing to pay my travel expenses from Spain, but hey ho. On the plane to Marbella that night I penned yet another letter to the chairman thanking him for allowing me to experience first hand the workings of the takeover panel, and told him that they did not want to see me again. I also laid out a plan for the change that I believed was necessary to return the company to profitability. Sadly it fell on deaf ears, and the company went into liquidation some years later. What a waste. I know I could have saved that business, the 400 jobs involved, and of course improved my own stake in the business by about 7:1. Back in Puerto Banus I was over it. During the next couple of months I made offers on three different land deals, each time being gazumped at the last minute. Property prices were just going mad over there at that time. It had been around nine months now since I had started golfing and partying most days and surprisingly I was starting to get sick of it. Moreover, I could sense that my brain was definitely slowing down with the alcohol and lack of activity. I decided over the next few weeks that I was too young to retire; it was probably doing me more harm than good. And so I booked the next plane out, to return to blighty. Once there I would figure out what I wanted to do.

10

BACK ON THE ACQUISITION TRAIL
1999 – 2006

Well, I had my rest and got tired. There is some irony there I think. I decided that if I was going back to work I would really go for it this time. I acquired 100% of the share capital and business assets of three companies during the following eighteen months. One of the companies was purchased from previous shareholders, and two were from administrators. All of a sudden I had gone from zero to £10 million turnover and some 200 employees whose mouths, and those of their families, I was responsible for feeding. Each acquisition was different (they always are), and thus the lessons learned also. I will outline the issues that arose and also introduce three more MBA models into this part of the story – the McKinsey 7 S Framework, the Ansoff Matrix, and Core Competencies.

TENBY PRECISION

I first saw the business advertised for sale in the *Financial Times*. It was a tooling manufacturer with sales around £2 million and thirty employees based near Nottingham. The raw material was tungsten carbide in powder form (an extremely hard material) which the company would sinter, effectively moulding and baking the powder in round or square forms before precision-machining them to tolerance limits of microns – very high precision. Customers, such as Tube Investments PLC, used this tooling for the production and extrusion of their steel golf shafts. Other companies, such as BSC, used this carbide tooling for its wear-resisting properties and thus longevity of tool life. So it served a number of companies in a number of industries and appeared to have its own niche.

The business was marginally profitable and the previous owner's reason for selling was that he'd taken it as far as he could. I visited the facility and it all looked in good order by and large. The general manager told me there wasn't much competition, just two companies in Birmingham, one in Daventry, one in Cardiff and one, mysteriously, in Sutton, south London. All (other than Sutton) were based near steel works or the metal stamping industries which they served. The only other competitor that was able to 'sinter' the raw powder into mould form was the Sutton company. Furthermore, the manager believed that the Welsh and London companies, both owned by ageing shareholders, were themselves available for purchase. Interesting, I thought. Was there a consolidation play here? Maybe I could buy up a few competitors and so gain decent market share and then potentially have greater control of prices and profits over time – worth further consideration. The company had also just received some export orders from Germany, driven in part by the weak pound, and this might prove to be an opportunity.

Thus I contacted, and visited the London and Cardiff companies. They were indeed for sale but at what price? I parked it for now as I had not even agreed terms on Tenby Precision as yet. The next day I tried to rationalise the opportunity. **One of the MBA models that I used to help me think it through was the Ansoff Matrix.**

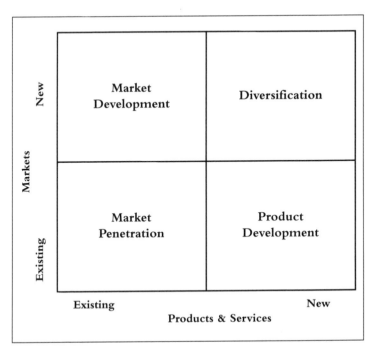

Figure 11. Ansoff Matrix

The Ansoff Matrix was first published in the Harvard Business Review in 1957. Its beauty is its simplicity, and it can help users to think about growth or development opportunities.

MARKET DEVELOPMENT
(Existing Products / New Markets)

- Target different markets, at home or abroad
- Use different sales channels, maybe online.

DIVERSIFICATION
(New Products / New Markets)

- This is a high risk strategy – delving into the unknown.
- An advantage might be, to spread a portfolio of risk, as 'not all eggs in one basket'.

MARKET PENETRATION
(Existing Products / Existing Markets)

- This is trying to sell more of the same things, to the same people.
- Could launch a major advertising/promotion programme.
- Increase sales force, and thus representation presence.
- Buy a competitor company, (particularly in mature markets).

PRODUCT DEVELOPMENT
(New Products / Existing Markets)

• Develop new products.
• Improve existing product offering.

Thinking this through, for Tenby Precision's post acquisition strategy I could visualise two areas which would improve the business. Market development (I could employ a sales agent in Germany to take advantage of our lower prices and increase sales in mainland Europe) and market penetration (I could buy one or both of the competitors). Alongside this I forecast the company's (as it stood now) future profits and free cash flow. I calculated the four years future cash flow and this would be the maximum I would offer. It would be my walk away figure. Of course my first bid was much less than this, and after the usual posturing and haggling I purchased the business at under three years free cash flows. The deal was struck. Now down to work.

The first day I met all the employees, explained my broad rationale for the business, and then for the first few days sat back and observed. That old chestnut, culture, was the major issue. The atmosphere, pace of work (or lack of it) and self motivation was awful. Even worse, the general manager was likewise entrenched and thought this was normal practice. No wonder the profits were marginal. The next few months went by and new productivity and incentive targets were introduced along with a new sales agent in Germany. Meanwhile, alongside trying to change the culture, I had opened dialogue with the two competitors to see if further acquisition made sense. It didn't. The Cardiff company's balance sheet showed it to be virtually insolvent, and their premises and equipment had not seen investment for decades. I was not interested, and they staggered on. The Sutton company, because of its location, had recently been offered a significant sum of money for the site they were on. They simply knocked the business down and built a new supermarket, so at least one was out of the way. After about six months things were improving slowly when another opportunity presented itself.

ADROIT PRECISION

This business had been put in the hands of an Administrator who had decided to make all the employees redundant shortly after its appointment by the company's bankers. One of the company's main customers, whom I had known in previous business, telephoned me to explain their concern about continuation of their supplies from Adroit. Would I go and have a look to see if I could help.

The company manufactured precision components for the aerospace industry. They were typically carved out of blocks of aluminium or titanium into complex shapes and tight tolerances, which were used in the production of aeroplanes and helicopters. Adroit had been part of a group, and the group was getting the blame for the failure from all around. I was not so sure having studied the family tree of the business. It had eleven directs and eleven indirects, a 1:1 ratio. Wow, man to man marking. This just couldn't be right. The company was based in Luton, had turnover of £1.5 million, and had 22 employees who were looking for a lifeline.

ADMINISTRATION, RECEIVERSHIP, LIQUIDATION

Putting a company into administration is sometimes instigated by the directors and/or shareholders who may wish to wind the company up voluntarily. But more often than not it is actioned by banks that have loaned the company money, and are not receiving their repayments because the company is insolvent. On any loan document from a High Street bank there will almost certainly be a clause that enables them to appoint an administrator or receiver to recover money owed to them. Alongside this they will register a first charge on all and any future assets at Companies House for all to see. This process then properly legalises the charge and puts them in front of any other creditor who has claims on the company.

The administration process is a kind of 'holding process' that effectively freezes creditor litigation or winding up orders for non-payment. This then gives the administrator time to analyse the situation and provide the best outcome for the creditors as a whole. He may try to sell the business as a going concern and achieve the best price possible to share among the company's creditors. Once this process has passed then the company will eventually go into liquidation, as it is normally only the trade and assets that are sold.

The people now licensed and regulated by the DTI (Department of Trade and Industry) are known as Insolvency Practitioners. I had met many during my career and these types generally did not sit well within the general confines of accountancy firms. They are not the normal straight laced, tick all the boxes type. They have to be more flexible, quick witted, devious and wily. Think of the love child of Del Boy and Angela Merkel and you're on the right track. So when I sat in the reception area of Adroit awaiting to meet (for the first time) the partner he did not let me down. He was dressed like an undertaker and, as usual, arrogant as they come. He proceeded to lecture me on his holier than thou duties to the creditors while I listened humbly, thinking that once they are appointed their order of priority is:

- **They get paid first, and as much as they can without upsetting the DTI.**
- **Ensuring the bank or chargeholder gets paid in full (because that's who gives them their next job).**
- **It would be nice if there was a bit left for all other creditors.**

He had, he explained, closed the business a few days earlier, made all the employees redundant, and was in the process of informing all the current debtors and creditors of the company. He was inviting offers for the assets of the business, and expected these within seven days. The assets comprised plant, machinery, stock, orders on hand, goodwill, trademarks and patents. He expected six interested parties to make a final offer. Well at least I knew where I stood.

That morning I spoke at some length to the previous manager of the company to find out what was wrong (the 1:1 Indirect/Direct ratio had given me a clue). He felt the group had managed them poorly for a number of years and that the shop floor directs were the best in the area whilst the support staff were more hindrance than support. More importantly I could see this guy really cared. He was passionate about the company and its customers – he had been there for twenty years. I then quizzed their sales manager about the business and its prospects. He was keeping all the existing customers informed of events and felt that provided the company could be resurrected quickly they could all be retained.

But what was it about the company that would enable it to become viable? After all it had no product of its own, it was merely a sub contractor. I started to consider another MBA model to help me think this through, the Core Competence of the company. This model developed by Prahalad and Hamel in 1990 analysed the competences and uniqueness within companies which would aid their survival and future growth. They broke down the test for true competences into three areas:

- **RELEVANCE**
  The competence must strongly influence the customer to continually purchase.

- **DIFFICULTY OF IMITATION**
  The competence should be difficult to imitate, otherwise the competition will do so.

- **BREADTH OF APPLICATION**
  The competence should open up other markets to aid growth.

Figure 12. Core Competence model. Prahalad and Hamel

Talking to the managers of Adroit I asked a critical question, 'why do customers select Adroit, and why do they keep coming back?' This would tackle the relevance issue. After some discussion it seemed that price, quality, service were a given in its industry. If you did not compete in these areas, then you were dead anyway. But Adroit figured its key strength, was flexibility and *excellent* service to its customers. Of course everyone talks about it and thinks they do it, but few truly do. And it is difficult to *imitate* properly. It is about having the right organisational structure, the right culture, the right mindset and above all people who *care* about customers and their daily issues. They cited some examples and I was convinced. Could this competence open up other markets? I didn't care at this point; I just knew I had to buy it.

Back to the undertaker's office. I made him an offer he could not refuse (no, not the horse's head in the bed). I wrote out a cheque for the full and fair value of the assets, as detailed by a valuing agent, which was open for twenty four hours, after which the offer would lapse and I would (I bluffed) proceed to do some of the ex-company's customers' work at my other facility, as they were concerned for supply to their own production. Twenty four hours; he didn't wait 24 seconds, we agreed the deal subject to contract.

It is important to understand that when you purchase assets in this way that all the risks are the buyer's. The administrator's contract of sale will normally give no warranties whatsoever if things go wrong. For example, once all the assets are purchased and paid for, a finance company may appear, claiming ownership of a machine you have already paid for. A creditor may appear with a valid retention of title claim and repossess the stock you have purchased. So great care is needed before you commit, as you have no warranties.

The deal was done within seven days. I had moved the assets into premises a third of the size and a third of the cost too. I employed eleven of the previous 22 employees, one sales manager and ten directs including a working manager, a new ratio of Indirects/Directs of 10:1. We retained all the customers and produced the same turnover of £1.5 million from the new facility. After all the upheaval of moving, month two showed a profit, and I was able to witness a truly flexible and caring team with a positive attitude that wanted the company to succeed. Ten years on I am still the proud owner of this business, and it has expanded steadily over time. We have taken on more people who fit the company's culture, and we have had the odd retirement, but in ten successful years there, none of the 'originals' has left I am delighted to say. Barely had the ink dried on this deal when I was made aware of another engineering company that had gone into administration, Incan Precision based in Harlow, Essex.

INCAN PRECISION

The company manufactured large press tooling (used to press out the lids of Coca Cola cans), and associated precision-machined parts for the canning and drinks packaging industry. The customer base was worldwide and the business employed about sixty people with annual sales of around £4 million before it entered administration. The company's directors were the 100% shareholders. They had purchased the company four years previously as a management buy out. The bank had pulled the plug after the company suffered a large bad debt, some small continuing losses, and the shareholders had shown reluctance to pledge any further security for the bank's loans to the company. The bank had decided to appoint administrators.

I went to meet the two previous directors. The sales director was an engineering graduate from Cambridge

University and the other was acting as managing director. And so their story was one of, in their own words, bad luck. They continued to describe how good the business was, the opportunities and so on. On touring the shop I felt unconvinced. The few workers who had been retained by the administrator looked sullen to say the least. The line managers were less than complimentary about the directors; there was just no harmony. However it was a time of shock and stress all around, so maybe these were just reactions of naturally disappointed people.

That night I wondered whether to proceed any further. Would the company fit with Tenby and Adroit Precision? Could they cross-fertilise their respective customer bases, and maybe centralise the sales and accounting functions and so on? There were about a dozen interested parties left after the administrator had sorted out the wheat from the chaff which, as ever, included advisors, brokers, accountancy firms and so on.

I called another meeting with the ex-directors. If I were to take this on someone had to manage it, so I threw them an offer. If they personally put in their own money then I would offer them 12.5% of the company each, leaving me with 75% of the business (and full control). They jumped at it, I guess buoyed by the fact that they would be back in full employment. And so I put in our offer. As usual, there were many twists and turns, with the administrator being abnormally difficult or perhaps I should say 'normally' as in my experiences. Finally a deal was agreed, and the cheque was paid. A week later I sold off some surplus plant and equipment to recoup half of my investment.

A new budget was set, with an incentive plan for increases above budget. The culture going forward was the philosophy that the budget equals employment, above budget means rewards, and gradually things started to improve. All three companies started to cross-trade rather than giving work as previously to outsiders. The two directors seemed to be doing an OK job with some guidance in certain areas when out of the blue I received a phone call from Hooley Holdings PLC, one of Incan's competitors. Their chairman explained that they hadn't been able to register a bid in time for the administrator because of all the PLC rigmarole, but he had been tracking us for the last eight months to see how things were. We arranged a meeting. It was simple. He offered double what I had paid for the company eight months previously, in cash, now. Furthermore he agreed to keep on all the employees as well as the two directors. The deal was signed within a week and I banked a big fat cheque. A bit of luck? Sure was, but I guess it evens out both ways over life. And that was the end of Incan as I knew it.

During this period, I had been approached by a company's chairman to see if I would be interested in purchasing a company from the ageing shareholders of RollCold. One door closes and another opens.

ROLLCOLD 2000

The company was a manufacturer of sections to the automotive, white goods and heavy vehicle industries, sunroof frames, shower frames, cooker hob frames for example. It had annual turnover of around £4 million and seventy employees based in the South East. The business was owned by two elderly gentlemen who simply wanted to retire. The company had been established over for 25 years and had always been profitable, but marginally so. After an initial review of the business, and the shareholders' expectations on price, I agreed to conduct some due diligence to see if I could match their requirements. The deal was never going to be straightforward as the shareholders were hell bent on ensuring that they maximised their own tax position in any potential deal. As matters progressed I agreed to become a paid consultant to the company, working a day a week for three months in order to get a full inside assessment. That's what I call full disclosure to a potential buyer, quite unusual.

During this period a deal was thrashed out that suited them and me. I had worked out that if all went reasonably well I would get my money back in three years. The company had muddled on for a number of years with no real strategy, plan or proper organisation from what I could see. The chairman was 80 years old and attended only now and then. The long standing managing director had died recently. This left some functional heads who had grown up with the business to do their daily routine, but with little guidance about which direction they should all be pointing. The systems used within the business were not integrated at all as the functional heads were going their own way regarding support software and reporting packages.

I started to think through some of the issues in hand and another MBA model came to mind, the McKinsey 7 'S' model:

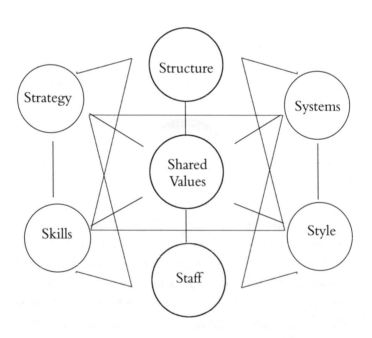

Figure 13. McKinsey 7 'S' model

Let's look at each of the elements specifically:

- **Strategy**: the plan devised to maintain and build competitive advantage over the competition.
- **Structure**: the way the organization is structured, and who reports to whom.
- **Systems**: the daily activities and procedures that staff members engage in to get the job done.
- **Shared Values**: called "superordinate goals" when the model was first developed these are the core values of the company that are evidenced in the corporate culture and the general work ethic.
- **Style:** the style of leadership adopted.
- **Staff:** the employees and their general capabilities.
- **Skills:** the actual skills and competencies of the employees in the company.

Within the seven elements there are three hard elements (Strategy, Structure, Systems) and four soft elements (Shared values, Skills, Style, Staff), these softer issues being more touchy feely.

Thinking through these elements with the management team helped us to develop a future vision and shared values. The first step, as always for me, was to build a strategy on the basis of, Where we are now? Where do we want to be? And how are we going to get there? We quickly rationalised that as a high volume parts producer we were continually under threat from foreign and particularly Chinese competition. It would be impossible to compete on price, so we decided that we wanted to become the most flexible and most excellent service provider. We would need to make it easy for our customers to deal with us and enjoy the experience.

We then went through the organisational structure to support our mantra, appointing specific people to be the main champion of our new customer focus. The systems were reviewed to ensure that we complemented our customers' systems and we introduced electronic invoicing to make it easy to order from us. Step by step we went through the process, aligning all the 7 'S' model elements to form a new set of shared values and culture for the company. We documented this and that became the way forward for the company.

The years flew by and things were improving slightly despite the continual pressure on prices. Leyland Daf Vehicles managed to go bust on me for a second time, this time for £40,000 compared to the previous £70,000. LDV was then resurrected for the third time and someone there phoned me with a problem. A rolled section manufacturer in the midlands had gone bust and LDV's tools and components were there, putting their entire van production output in jeopardy. Oh well – a chance to get my money back I thought. And so I went off to this supplier, Whitehouse. When I got there I found that they had their own product range, electrical trunking rolled sections in steel, which they sold to lighting trade sheds such as Newey and Eyre. Interesting. I wondered if we could then have our own product range to safeguard our future business. So on a whim, and to keep LDV happy, I purchased the entire assets of the business that day. The lorry loads of machines started arriving at base and we took temporary storage. We also successfully integrated the extra business from LDV into the factory. And then once the dust had settled we looked into the market prices for this electrical trunking – bloody awful. And so on another whim I resold the electrical trunking business to a business in that trade. It was only a small transaction, and we still turned a small profit. It was sad to see this business go but sometimes you just have to give things a go. Life if full of prescriptions but if you're doing nothing, there's nothing doing.

Another few years flew by and we were in 2004. We had been reasonably profitable for the previous four years, but changes in price competition and the difficulty in obtaining new work (by now one of our major customers, Electrolux, was sourcing from India and China) was making life continually difficult. Then in the summer of 2004 we were dealt some hammer blows in quick succession. Three of our major customers decided to place all their future work in India, China and Taiwan. Then LDV went bust on me again, for a third time, owing us £80,000. And collection of money owed became increasingly difficult as customers started to cling on to their (our) money for longer. The picture looked bleak. The atmosphere around the company darkened as everybody could see the daily order intake and the future schedules were dwindling. I had felt around November time that we would have no choice but to close the business despite having over £250,000 in the company's bank account at the time.

However, one of the company's customers was having trouble in China and they offered a few months' work which would keep us viable into the New Year. I jumped at it. Meanwhile continual talks were being held between the works management, shop floor and unions to prepare for the worst in the months ahead.

Four years prior to this I had refused to talk to the company's shop stewards and their own Unite local office representative ever again. I have always enjoyed excellent relationships with unions and employees throughout my career. But these individuals I felt were in it for themselves. The meeting ended there and then, and thereafter all future meetings were held with the works management team. Thus when the inevitable time came to close the company, despite everybody being kept informed, fully paid up to date, and treated with the best respect possible in the circumstances, the unions turned to Unite claiming that a longer notice period was required. Of course our own company lawyers had advised throughout the process on this, and all other matters. It was a stressful time for all.

The very next day, after I had informed everybody that the business was closing, a man dressed as a postman lurked outside my home. I was at work at the time, it was 8 am.

This postman then trespassed into my office at work, and after asking me to sign for a letter revealed himself to be a *Daily Mirror* reporter. I was stunned. He then led a rapid-fire question session about the company closure. I offered the *Daily Mirror* a proper interview if they so wished in proper circumstances, not an ambush. I telephoned the editor that day and complained bitterly. It fell on deaf ears. The next day the *Daily Mirror* just printed what it wanted to, sensationalised rubbish. And they managed to get a mention on Radio Two. A spat then ensued between me, my lawyer, the *Daily Mirror* editor and Unite. Libel lawyers unfortunately start at £500,000; I wasn't upset that much.

I think this was a lesson in how quickly the media can pounce and sensationalise events. I do not believe that these actions are helping Britain to get back on its feet. There will be thousands of entrepreneurs out there looking to start businesses, risking their own money and creating jobs, but would they do that if people act unreasonably. I doubt it very much.

Despite this I had spent over five generally happy years with the company and its numerous characters. There were many challenges along the way and I would like to share one of them regarding business law with you.

A LESSON IN GOING LEGAL

I had owned the business for some years and generally had got to know the managers quite well. Our purchasing manager had kept a tidy ship, and so I was surprised when on one of my weekly visits to the company he presented me with a problem. He had given a purchase order to a supplier for one million special rivets to be delivered in accordance with our monthly schedule. This total supply was to be spread over approximately four years, 250,000 special rivets per annum. He had used this supplier many times before, so the supplier knew of our business and, importantly, potential changes to product design and modification.

There was indeed a product change, and therefore no need for this special rivet. The order was then duly cancelled and we accepted a future three months delivery liability as detailed on the company's delivery schedule which was sent to the supplier each month. However, unbeknown to us this supplier had taken a 'flier'. They had gone to China and had all one million rivets made in one go, four years supply at a very low cost, compared to the agreed selling price to us. They were threatening to sue us and wanted payment for the total order at the full selling price – and that's why it now landed on my desk.

I reviewed the paperwork trail with the purchasing manager and played devil's advocate to see if there were any reasons for us not to cancel and accept liability. The paperwork seemed about 95% right (you can always find some fault if you really want to), so I arranged a meeting with the supplier to try to agree a way forward or find a compromise. Before the meeting they contracted a 'no win, no fee' lawyer to take on their case. The meeting thus proved fruitless because of their intransigence. The total full claim from them was a mere £9,050. The position of our own purchasing manager was equally intransigent. He was most indignant about the whole matter and told the supplier he would never deal with them again (an annual loss of business worth some £100,000).

Still, the 'no win, no fee' lawyer decided to sue. I was torn between backing my management or just paying this irritation off to get it out of the way. I decided to consult my lawyers, a prestigious midlands law firm, that certainly knew how to charge. The partner there, having looked at the paperwork trail, concluded that there was no case to answer. Given my previous experiences of litigation I by now always asked lawyers the chances of winning or losing a case. Normally, given inherent risks, the answer is always fifty – fifty. In this case I was given ninety – ten in our favour. They believed it was a no-brainer. The downside would be their costs, estimated at around £30,000, just to get ready for the High Court. However, if we won the case we may get certain costs back and they reassured me that we would indeed win.

Given the total claim was only £9,050 I was still torn about what to do. I did feel that the company had done no wrong though and so let the litigation get started. I just had to back my management team.

Since the Wolffe reforms on litigation all parties were

supposed to act more reasonably during their efforts to tear limbs off each other. This involves notice letters, typically fourteen days to do this or else. There is then a period of what is known as discovery, where each party's lawyers describe their case and then exchanging their defence or prosecution with each other. At an early stage a judge is appointed to preside over the case. At every stage all the correspondence or bickering along the way is set before him. This gives him a good insight into the issues before the trial. During this discovery period the court will set a trial date, and the judge will be formally assigned to preside. The high court hearing was set for four months time, at Milton Keynes.

After a few months and much paper the judge called a pre-trial hearing. It is the process of ensuring that both parties are indeed ready for trial, and of course enabling yet another opportunity for both parties to settle and stop wasting the court's time. The eminent law firm representing us remained adamant: we will not settle, we cannot lose. I went along with them on this. At this point a barrister is required to advocate our case at trial and our lawyer recommended one of its own in house barristers, a solicitor advocate it was called. Their rationale was that we would benefit from a close working environment, ease of communication and so on. I was then shown his CV and it was, on paper, very impressive. He was not around at present, and I was about to go on holiday for four weeks, so I just ran with it.

A few days before the case I made sure that I was back to

attend. Before this I had a few calls from the partner handling the case, and one from the barrister. They seemed very confident and would not even question the company's witnesses (purchasing manager) until the day, relying for now on his own affidavit, sworn statement, already presented to the court. The very day before the trial the presiding judge who had followed the case from the beginning could not hear the case. Worse, the court had offered to reassign the case to Wolverhampton with an entirely new judge. My advisers accepted it. I was just told that it would be OK and I accepted their advice.

I arrived at the high court and met our barrister for the first time. First impressions, unimpressive, and you never get a second chance to make a first impression. I asked him why he hadn't met our two witnesses before now to prepare but he was adamant that the case, as far as the paper trail was concerned, was so strong that there was no need. When I pushed him a bit harder I noticed a strange reaction. He started to clam up, worse he had a slight stammer. Must be pre-trial nerves I thought. Moments later the two main company witnesses entered the room for a pre-trial chat, thirty minutes before the hearing. Things started to worsen. One of our key witnesses was dressed in a black suit, dark grey shirt and black tie, like a 1930s gangster. Still, style and taste for fashion should be invisible to the law you would hope.

The trial started and the judge entered the courtroom and shuffled his way to the bench. He must have been at least

75 years old. He opened the case and asked each party for their pleas. I could almost sense that this guy could not be bothered. Here he was, assigned a brand new case the night before, with two sides squabbling over £9,000. It wasn't worthy of his court, I could sense from his body language. On this point alone, he was right.

Our barrister, who was wigless, stood up and stammered his way through his plea. The judge (and opposing barrister) who were both wigged and gowned was more interested in where his wig was rather than the defence. The chap then tried to explain that as a solicitor advocate he was not obliged to wear one. Well, this judge felt he should do, irrespective of any new way. It was not a good start.

Both sides then presented their cases, leaving the judge looking a mixture of confused, bemused and almost half asleep. He concluded at that he did not know who was right, but the mere fact that the supplier had made all the parts must mean that they were right. We had lost. Worse, my costs would be our lawyer's fees and all our opponents' costs, £78,000 in total from an initial argument over £9,050. Our lawyers were dumbfounded, although not so dumbfounded that they agreed to reduce their own fees at all. This, despite stammering barrister boy with no wig, and them bypassing the maxim 'fail to plan: plan to fail'. We fell out forever, and I paid the bill.

This true story should serve as a reminder both when choosing advisors and taking on the law. Only do it as a last resort. And looking back the other side's advisors were on a 'no win, no fee' agreement. Did this make them hungrier than mine? You bet it did.

11

OUT OF THE ASHES: 2006 – TODAY

The business was first advertised in the *Financial Times*. It was in administration and offers were invited for the assets of the company. The company Brauer was the market leader in clamps and wheels, and had been in existence in different forms for eighty years. The products were exported to forty countries around the globe with sales revenues of some £5 million. It was based in Milton Keynes and had around sixty employees.

The administrators were on site and running the business as a going concern for now. These guys were actually human, and you could have a proper discussion with them, a novelty. As always in an on site administration the noise level was high with phones continually ringing. Suppliers, the landlord and finance companies were all hastily trying to get the latest information to see how their own vested interests were faring. The employees were clinging to the administrators who immediately after the court's appointment had effectively become the new managing director of the company, and hence the powerhouse. Confusion, disarray and misinformation abounds in these circumstances, not a pretty sight.

I had a brief discussion with the (very soon to depart) managing director (who looked like he'd been in hell) before interviewing the management team there. The sales manager, in particular, impressed me with his knowledge of the business, customers and future prospects. He impressed me even more when he offered to put some of his own personal money into a new venture to salvage the business. But what was wrong? Was the business a viable proposition? Why did it really go under? Who would run the business going forward? The company had been part of a group and the group had also gone down – so, of course, the group had been blamed by all and sundry as usual. After touring the facility I realised that part of the problem was staring me in the face, literally eyeball to eyeball. There were actually more chiefs than Indians.

The sales manager confirmed that he knew that the company was top heavy (with temporary staff and some impending retirements this would change the profit forecasts significantly).

But what about prices? He confirmed that prices to American and far east customers had been held for three years on the insistence of the previous owner. He felt that they could be raised by 10% without losing any future business, which was encouraging.

But what about future growth? He confirmed that the wheels business had of late moved into the offshore wind farm industry. The company had developed wheel systems that sit on board a ship underneath a carousel that would unwind cabling at sea (like an umbilical cord) to the actual windmill. He believed this to be a growing market.

But did he really want to put his own money in for 25% share, and could he really run the business? Yes, he would definitely put the money in and he would have a go at running it. By then I was convinced I would do the deal if the price was right, and only if I would get a full payback in around four years.

I spent the next three days talking to the landlord (future lease of the premises), finance companies (who owned the machines), banks (on future finance), the employees (to allay their fears and get them onside), some key customers (to build their future confidence) and some key suppliers (to understand their issues on money they had lost, stock they held and to build some bridges for the future). A hectic three days but I had, in principle, got agreement in all these key areas to enable the business to go forward. A deal was done. The sales manager put his money where his mouth was, and took over the reins of the business, owning 25% of it. After a short induction period of a few months helping him to execute the plan we'd first dreamt up in his office just before the deal, I was able to retreat completely, just the way I like it, and let him get on and develop the business.

The company was profitable in month two and has remained so ever since.

TODAY 2011

And through all the melee here we are today. I tend to look after Adroit holdings which does some trading but essentially is the purse strings, while the managing directors continue to run and develop Adroit Precision and Brauer, in which they both hold equity stakes. The annual turnover of the businesses today is around £8 million with healthy profits.

We have migrated, along with many others in the UK, into niche businesses predominantly through necessity. Simply put, we have generally become too expensive in the UK to produce high volume products any more. We just can't, at present, compete with China for example on price. If we want to retain our high living standards, and the generally low unemployment levels enjoyed in this country over the last four decades, then UK PLC will need a first class, properly trained and educated workforce.

LESSONS LEARNED ALONG THE WAY

As I said at the beginning of this book, I have a great interest in the development of education in general, and the management and running of businesses in particular. I believe that everyone living in this country owes it to themselves, their families and their country to continually better themselves. What better way to start than further education, and what easier way to start than the Open University, that great institution that has enabled so many people to change their lives? I hope I may have inspired some of you to want to join their MBA programme, or any other learning programme.

PEOPLE

In virtually every business (unless you have some unique patented invention) people are the key attribute. People make it happen, or not, as the case may be. However, people need to feel safe, they need guidance, they crave leadership that makes them feel secure. Remember Maslow's Hierarchy of Needs. And they need to feel loved, wanted and, importantly, that they are impressing someone. It is a true leader who can satisfy the needs of the people within the business and direct them all towards the company's aims.

There is a lot of talk about lean processes and lean thinking and these *are* important management techniques. However, in my experience a fired up, motivated team of ten people under a truly effective leader can do the work of twenty people working under an ineffective one. Yes, that's a 100% productivity increase. If people are left to their own devices they will generally expand their work to the time allowed, not the most effective use of time. Leadership is the key.

THE WAY FORWARD

The most common excuse for someone not doing or

starting something is that they don't have the time. While undoubtedly this is true in some circumstances, in many others it is just that, an excuse.

If someone wants to do an MBA then they have to find a way, whatever the obstacles in their path. I managed to complete it part-time while still running and managing my companies. Another lady on my course had a senior role in the NHS and a young family of four children. She managed her workload by setting her alarm at 3 am and then studying for two hours before getting a couple of hours more sleep and then going to work. Another colleague had started a one year business studies course before doing a two year management course and then taking another four years to complete his part-time MBA. My point here is that if you really want to do it, you can find a way. It may take 10 years, so the sooner you start the better. Moreover, the journey along the way will be interesting and make your life richer.

In some ways the same goes for starting or buying a business. You really have got to *want* to do it. Of course initial start up capital of some sort will be necessary, but that needn't deter you. History tells us that there is always capital available somewhere for a good idea, provided you don't give up.

And there is no reason not to start in a much smaller way with very limited risk or initial capital outlay. For example, designing greetings cards or baking speciality cakes at home to your own designs or recipes, and selling them on market stalls can be a good way to start. Look how Marks and Spencer started at their penny bazaar stalls. The challenge of starting a business *can* be daunting but you can start in this very small way.

I have found that the necessary attributes to enable you to run a business successfully are the ability to get on with and motivate people; persistence; tenacity; desire; attitude; drive, and importantly nous – that mystical ability to spot an opportunity and make a profit from it. If you possess or can acquire those qualities you are already half way there.

As far as the MBA is concerned there is little risk and enormous benefit to be gained through educating oneself in the business world. Let's face it, money makes the world go round. So the more informed you are the clearer you will see the ever-changing business world. And this can be started with a simple trip to the library.

So are you going to be one of the 'I haven't got time' brigade, or are you going to do something to not only improve your life but help many others too?

12

LEADERSHIP AND THOUGHTS FOR THE FUTURE

LEADERSHIP

Management and business, like many other things in life, go through their own fads and fashion. The latest 'hot topic' is leadership, in particular 'are leaders made or born'? It's that old chestnut again, the Nurture or Nature leadership question. I will explain my own view on this question based purely upon my own personal experiences.

Nature throws up all sorts in life and we kind of just accept it as the norm; that we are all born differently – different abilities, needs, wishes, desires to name a few. It is as though this acceptance is in our very own culture, as this has been the way for centuries.

Brilliant and gifted people from all walks of life are born: golf – Jack Nicklaus; football – Pele; music – Bach or Beethoven; science – Einstein; humanity – Gandhi, Nelson Mandela – amongst many others. We generally accept that these people were born gifted and in their own way are leaders as well as being 'the best'.

Undoubtedly through their own lives they continued (and some still do) to develop and improve their own craft. However, without being born with the initial capability, they could not (no matter how hard they tried) become the best.

In the same way the great leaders of the business world (in my view) were *born* with the capability to lead – think Jack Welch – General Electric; Lee Iacocca – Chrysler; Lord Weinstock – Marconi.

Underneath these titans, whether in sport, music, science or indeed business, are the next level of performers and so forth downwards. These differing levels will each lead and manage their own situations accordingly. All levels still need leadership whether it is a country, company, department, section and so on.

The leadership traits that I believe people are born with (undoubtedly at varying levels) are as follows:

- Leaders as a first must provide *dignity* and respect for all around, no matter whom.
- They are *driven* and *focussed* to achieve the task ahead.
- They are able to explain *simply* the task to others and *delegate* effectively.
- They are able to *influence* and *manage* the teams towards the *goal*.
- They engender *respect* and are *trusted* by those they lead.

- They provide *inspiration* and help *develop* those around to better themselves.
- They are good *listeners* and continually *review* the *process* upon feedback from all around attain the goal.
- They possess *determination* and *persistence* in spades.
- They display *enthusiasm, humility* and *modesty*.
- They have an inherent 'chameleon-like' ability to change as the *circumstance* demands to become *difficult, tough, humorous, ruthless.*

Well, there are a lot of capabilities there. Look at the words:

Dignity, respect, driven, focussed, achieve, simply, delegate, influence, manage, goal, respect, trust, inspiration, develop, listeners, review, process, determination, persistence, humility, modesty, circumstance, difficult, enthusiasm, tough, humorous, ruthless.

Can any one person really have *all* these attributes? Yes, I believe the truly great leaders do, and at a very high level.

Nature will only yield a number of these talented types it seems. However, many others with differing levels of the above capabilities will be born and will be perfectly able to lead their own, but probably lower level, companies. They will then, over time, be able to develop their leadership qualities further, for example, to become a better listener or manage processes better and so on.

For many decades now (as part of the employment process for senior managers) psychometric and personality tests have been used. You will recall in (Chapter 4) that I personally undertook extensive tests at that time at job interviews. The purpose of the tests being to try and predict the suitability of applicants for the role to be filled.

Despite all these screenings/tests, history is littered with failed MD's after 18 or so months in the job. It is not easy. The business world is rarely predictable – here is why a number of things can change the picture.

- The business world is complex and continually changing.
- Businesses go through different phases – start up, development, cash problems etc.
- People change through life – team problems, personal problems.
- Customers change. Markets change.
- Internal politics and power struggles come into play.

It is a dynamic situation.

So companies requiring leaders need to be *very* clear on where the company is *now* and where it *wants to go to*. This is the very first step, before even considering the attributes of a leader needed to take the company forward. Unfortunately the business world is rarely that simple as less admirable human traits tend to take over – such as politics, greed, envy, power – and these then become yet further variables within the process.

My own simplistic view on how to select a leader for a company would be to carefully consider what the company's wants, needs, desires are. Then to ensure that such wishes are achievable, and deliverable, in the real world with the resources available.

Just using two sheets of paper, list on one sheet the company's plans/targets etc. Whilst on the other sheet list the skills and attributes necessary from the 'target leader' to achieve those plans. Then at interview, ask each candidate to demonstrate in the 'real world' how they have previously displayed such attributes successfully. Then check the chemistry, personality and the candidate's own 'cultural fit' – and go with your heart.

Coming back to my own leadership experiences in life, from the age of five, I recall displaying some leadership qualities, as I became captain of the playground football team. I never particularly sought out this early recognition but it just somehow happened. I suspect my dear mother's endless work drive aided my personal development in those formative years. This would then have been developed further in my 'law of the jungle' school years. Learning the value of money in those early days, I believe also contributed towards being a better leader. It enabled the true understanding of the 'have' and 'have nots', and how good it felt to actually work and save hard to go and buy something that I had earned. This in turn, I believe, breeds humility, respect and dignity for all. A major attribute I believe which is essential for a true leader.

Early on in my career I was able to witness at first hand some truly remarkable leaders and this again helped my personal development significantly. The good ones were able to implement the 'carrot and stick' or inject 'fear' as the need or the circumstance arose. Of course many other situations require an arm around the shoulder, enthusiasm or coaching. This is why a leader has to be able to display so many different attributes in order to lead effectively. It is probably the most difficult task within business to get right.

And so, back to that old chestnut, 'are leaders born or made'. I think that I have demonstrated that it is my general feeling that they are born, but many, through personal development, can become very capable leaders. So I think my conclusion would be that it is a bit of both – sitting on the fence a bit. However, what I strongly believe is that the truly great leaders are most definitely *born*.

THOUGHTS FOR THE FUTURE

Since I started my career some 40 years ago the business world and the way in which business is carried out have changed enormously. Technological advances such as the internet, the ease of travel and the emergence of the BRIC countries (Brazil, Russia, India and China) have changed the business landscape hugely, and now we have a truly global market.

In many ways I have also personally had to adapt to meet these changes and ensure survival. In my own journey each stage from apprentice to engineer to manager and finally director has presented its own challenges.

My first turnaround, which seemed so daunting at the time, was *made* to work. Inner belief (or was it survival mode?) enabled my vision to become a reality. None of this would have been possible without that rare and most important of commodities, people working towards the common cause. And people will only do this for a prolonged length of time if you are fair and they believe in you.

The business world continues to change apace with competition becoming ever fiercer. Indeed during the last decade so much money, machinery and investment has gone to the Far East, particularly China, that the balance of power is tilting. China and India together make up nearly a third of the world's population (1.2 billion in China and one billion in India) and they are no longer prepared to accept poor living standards. They are hungry for jobs in business and we in the UK have a major challenge on our hands in order to compete. It is up to us all to play our part if we value our future generations' prosperity. If we do not then the rest of the world will take our jobs gladly, I am sure.

I have personally been through four business recessions in my career, starting with the Oil Crisis and the three day week of the early 1970s and witnessing the housing market bubbles, the Internet bubble of 2000 and now of course the credit crunch of 2008. Since the early 70s it has been the accepted wisdom that there would be a crash every 10 or so years. There were 15 or so years of good times in the build up to 2008. Many commentators have come up with their own theories on when the current recession will end. Some say we are in slow recession, some say it is a double dip recession, while others are less bullish altogether. My own view, and why I believe it is so necessary to further your own education or start a business for yourself, is this.

The world had some fifteen years of easy credit at ever-decreasing interest rates as the capital surpluses looked for buyers. Mortgage lending around the world became lax to say the least. The American sub prime market failures are now well documented. But closer to home my children's friends were getting 125% mortgages from Northern Rock and purchasing property, sometimes even without proof of future earnings. And so they would buy a property for £200,000 and receive £250,000 from Northern Rock minus expenses. With this extra money they purchased televisions, furniture, holidays and cars. This in turn created jobs around the world for people who supplied such products and services. Then the increased demand for housing pushed house prices even higher, making people feel even wealthier and encouraging them to take out further loans to purchase anything they desired. This massive global housing bubble which created a false market and false employment is at present deflating. Governments around the world are trying to ease the pain of unemployment by printing more money. I personally believe however that this will simply delay the inevitable and that unemployment will continue to rise to the 'real' level before the easy money created false employment.

I recall in the early 90s, we sat in the Sky Bar at the Hyatt Hotel in Tokyo debating the Japanese stock market and housing prices which were rocketing at the time. The Nikkei index was around 40,000 and companies were being valued at around 30 to 40 times their yearly earnings. That's over 40 years to get your money back. I thought then that it couldn't go on like that. It didn't. There was a crash and the Nikkei today languishes around the 10,000 mark and Japan has teetered on the edge of recession for nearly two decades.

I mention this recent history because never will it be more important for us and for future generations to try to make things happen and improve in any small way we can, whether this be through education or indeed starting a business. It will be the SMEs of the future that will be the lifeblood of the country's future prosperity.

Throughout this story I hope that I have passed on a little information that may be of use some day to somebody, whether a student, someone going into business, managers, or someone doing or considering an MBA. I would therefore like to conclude with a tribute to the most important asset of any business by far, its *people*. It is they who set the pace, build the culture, create the innovation, make it happen, create the opportunities and yes, make the profits at the end of the day. And customers (without which there is no business) in the long term will only deal with people that they want to deal with. To ensure that we, as UK plc, give ourselves a chance to be great again we need to take our best people and make them our teachers for future generations. In this way if we can nurture entrepreneurs, drive innovation, deliver new and exciting products, then we may have a chance of retaining the high standard of living enjoyed in the UK for the last five decades.

Finally, perhaps a quote from Einstein puts it all into perspective. He said:

Guard against preaching to young people success as the main aim, more important is the pleasure in work, its result and the value to the community.

I hope this book shares his vision in some small part, and wish you luck on your own personal journey for the future.

APPENDIX 1:

Business Models/Figures

Figure:

APPENDIX 2

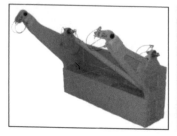

Adroit are a leading supplier to the Aerospace and Defence Industries of machined / fabricated components and assemblies.

We operate out of a modern manufacturing facility in Luton combining state of the art machining capabilities with the latest CATIA modelling software to produce high quality parts - on time for our blue chip customer base.

Quality approved to ISO9001 as well as Agusta Wesland, Rolls Royce and GKN Aerospace we manufacture in a wide variety of materials from titanium sheet to plastic rod to stainless steel plate and bar.

Adroit offers a complete project management service and a one stop manufacturing solution.

Adroit Precision Engineering Ltd.
Unit 5 Bilton Court, Bilton Way, Luton, Beds LU1-1LX
Phone;- 01582 411200. Fax;- 01582 411424
www.adroitaerospace.co.uk

APPENDIX 3

BRAUER®

The extensive range of Brauer products include, Wheels, Castors, Toggle Clamps, Airmovers and Standard Machine parts.

Brauer has more than 80 years design and manufacturing experience in the UK and along with an experienced design division can provide a comprehensive source of solutions for many engineering based projects.

If you cannot find a suitable product from within the standard range, Brauer can design and build to your own bespoke, drawing or specification.

Brauer manufactures wheel solutions as diverse as: ship transfer systems, offshore wind- turbine carousels, tunneling machinery, warehousing and retailing wheels.

Brauer is the European leader in Toggle clamping technology, with more than 400 different models to choose from and all available to design engineers in multi-format 2D & 3D CAD, drawing models, which are available for direct download from the Brauer web site.

Brauer Ltd also manufacture: Air Vacuum products, known as Airmovers, a range of products, which provide solutions to processes found in, food, pharmaceutical and chemical production, the applications, being: product conveying, fume, heat and particulate extraction and cooling of machines and processing equipment. In addition and within the process industry, Brauer also provides a full range of machinery supporting parts called: Standard Parts, which are fitted as handles, knobs and levers to process equipment and machinery.

Tel: 01908 374022 • Fax: 01908 641628

www.brauer.co.uk • email: sales@brauer.co.uk

APPENDIX 4

FURTHER SOURCES OF FREE USEFUL INFORMATION

Hopefully this book has inspired you to consider further your own business education. There is a wealth of free and useful business information from virtually every respectable business school in the world. This ranges from subject matters such as strategy through to general and current affairs. Some of the schools and their links are listed below for your convenience.

HARVARD UNIVERSITY – (USA)
www.hbsp.harvard.edu
http://athome.harvard.edu

THE MASSACHUSETTS INSTITUTE OF TECHNOLOGY – (USA)
http://ocw.mit.edu

INSEAD – (FRANCE)
http://knowledge.insead.edu/home.cfm

YALE UNIVERSITY – (USA)
http://opa.yale.edu/netcasts.aspx

CRANFIELD SCHOOL OF MANAGEMENT – (UK)
www.som.cranfield.ac.uk/som/executive.asp

BOSTON COLLEGE – (USA)
http://frontrow.bc.edu

INDEX